WIT & WISDOM of BASEBALL

SAUL WISNIA
WITH DAN SCHLOSSBERG

ILLUSTRATOR
ELIZABETH TRAYNOR

PUBLICATIONS INTERNATIONAL, LTD.

Louis Weber, C.E.O.
Publications International, Ltd.
7373 North Cicero Avenue
Lincolnwood, Illinois 60646

Manufactured in China

8 7 6 5 4 3 2 1

ISBN: 0-7853-2193-4

Library of Congress Card Catalog Number: 96-72655

Saul Wisnia, currently a book and website editor in Boston, is a former sports writer for *The Washington Post* and feature writer for *The Boston Herald*. His work has appeared in *Sports Illustrated, The Boston Globe, Boston Magazine,* and *The Boston Phoenix.* He was co-author of *Babe Ruth: His Life and Times* and *Baseball: More Than 150 Years* and a contributing writer to *The Best of Baseball, Treasury of Baseball,* and *Raging Bulls!* A former researcher/archivist for the Sports Museum of New England, he has also co-hosted a weekly Boston-area radio talk show. (Chapters 1-6)

Dan Schlossberg is baseball editor for the *American Encyclopedia Annual,* featured columnist for *Legends Sports Memorabilia,* and contributor to *Street & Smith's Official Baseball Yearbook* and *Bill Mazeroski's Baseball.* He also writes player profiles for Pinnacle baseball cards. His 17 books include *The Baseball Catalog, The Baseball Book of Why,* and *Total Braves.* The former Associated Press and United Press International sports writer is co-author of *Players of Cooperstown: Baseball's Hall of Fame.* (Chapter 7)

Photo Reference: Bradford Glazier

CONTENTS

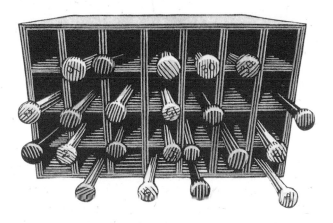

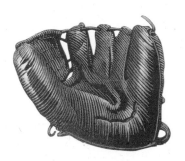

INTRODUCTION

"NEXT TO RELIGION, baseball has furnished
a greater impact on American life
than any other institution."

—HERBERT HOOVER

COMPARING THE TWO AMERICAN SPORTS of baseball and football, comedian George Carlin joked about the strategy employed to win at either game. "In football, the goal is to march into enemy territory with a series of hard smashes and long bombs and break through to pay dirt," he said brusquely. Then, conjuring up a silly grin, he squeaked: "In baseball, the object is to go home!"

His premise was that baseball lacked the cunning and manliness of football; that it was, in fact, a game for children rather than grownups. Such thinking might have earned Carlin a laugh, but a fundamental point was lacking in his analysis. The gridiron may be a place of greater physical dangers than the diamond, but no sport has a larger hold on the public consciousness or more impact on people of all ages than the national pastime. If football is warrior pitted against warrior, baseball is fathers playing catch with sons. The game is a tradition passed down from one generation to the next, and its finest performers and achievements remain as resoundingly American as the feats of great scholars and statesmen.

The proof is limitless. Baseball was played during breaks in battle by soldiers on both sides of the Civil War, and it is opening day and not the Super Bowl that all but one president since William Howard Taft has attended. When Ernest Hemingway needed a hero to keep Santiago going through his battle against the great fish in *The Old Man and the Sea*, he chose Joe DiMaggio—not Red Grange. Few remember what Magic Johnson said in his emotional retirement just a handful of years ago, yet the words of Lou Gehrig's farewell speech have been committed to memory for more than a half-century of repetition. Few basketball junkies know how many points Michael Jordan has scored over his career, or even his highest single-season average. However, ask the most casual of baseball followers the significance of the numbers 714 and 60, and you will likely get a quick response.

Baseball may indeed be slow, and its season long, but this allows those watching to appreciate the elements that make up each individual play. It is also why observations and quotations surrounding the game have become such an intricate part of its overall appeal. There is time to think in baseball, and therefore time to develop ritual and pathos and tradition. Yogi Berra said, "It ain't over till it's over." In between, there is plenty to notice.

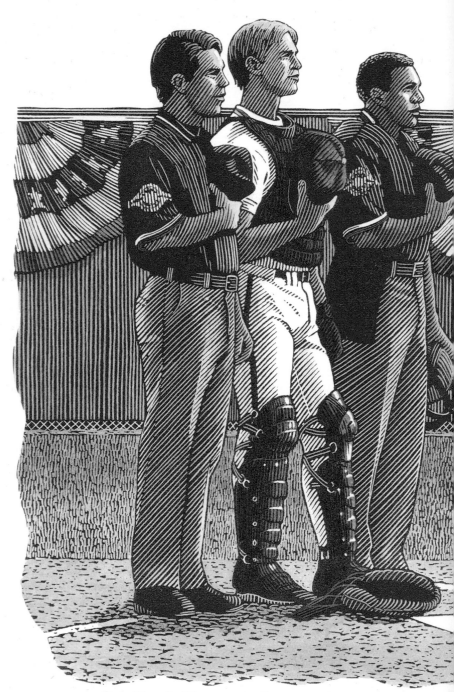

THE
AMERICAN
GAME

"SAY THIS MUCH for baseball—it is beyond question the greatest conversation piece ever invented in America."

—BRUCE CATTON, FASCINATING BASEBALL FACTS

THE DOUBLEDAY MYTH

WHEN A 1907 COMMISSION formed by A.G. Spalding set out to prove the true origins of baseball, there was little mention of previous versions of bat-and-ball games amidst patriotic praise for the supposed architect of "America's Game"— Major General Abner Doubleday. The story went that Doubleday, as a Cooperstown, New York, youngster in 1839, had drawn up a diagram of a diamond for a game he called "Town Ball." Conveniently, Doubleday later went on to heroics as the soldier who spotted the first gun fired at Fort Sumter, and was supposedly at Abe Lincoln's deathbed when the president leaned over and whispered in his ear, "Abner, don't . . . let . . . baseball . . . die."

A great story, but merely myth—especially considering Doubleday was actually at West Point in 1839 and was never known to even follow the game he supposedly invented. Still, Cooperstown proved a nice place to put the Hall of Fame.

"WHAT A BLESSING is conveyed by these
two words, base ball."

—PHILADELPHIA CITY ITEM, *1866*

"You can't tell the players without a scorecard."

—CONCESSIONAIRE HARRY M. STEVENS, LATE 19TH CENTURY

"The fundamental reason for the popularity of the game is the fact that it is a national safety valve. So long as it remains our national game, America will abide no monarchy, and anarchy will be too slow."

—ALLEN SANGREE, 1907

"A hot dog at the ballpark is better than steak at the Ritz."

—HUMPHREY BOGART, IN A FILM AD FOR ORGANIZED BASEBALL

"Whoever wants to know the heart and mind of America had better learn baseball, the rules and realities of the game."

—JACQUES BARZUN, PHILOSOPHY PROFESSOR, 1954

"Verily, the National Game is great!"

—SPORTING LIFE, 1884

PRESIDENTIAL PITCHIN'

ONE OF BASEBALL'S best-preserved traditions is that of the president throwing out the first ball of the season—a gesture that has come to symbolize everything patriotic about the game and has endured despite the departure of the Washington Senators for Texas. Fittingly, the first chief executive to perform the ritual was one of the most ardent fans ever to occupy the White House—William Howard Taft.

Taft was a chunky power hitter as a lad who some yarn-spinners claim was offered a big-league contract as a catcher by Cincinnati before throwing out his arm. The 300-pounder was on hand at Washington's Griffith Stadium on April 14, 1910, to take in the opener between the Senators and Athletics at the invitation of American League President Ban Johnson. Taft, the top-hatted tosser, removed his kid gloves and let loose with a low peg to Senators starter Walter Johnson. The Hall of Fame hurler went on to shut out the A's 3-0 on a one-hitter, and a tradition was born. Taft was back at Griffith to christen the 1911 season, and every president since except Carter has performed the feat at least once during office—even though the president now must travel to Baltimore to do so.

". . . THERE ARE TWO THINGS I teach the boys that are all American. One's the good old flag and one's baseball."

—SPORTS WRITER TIM MURNANE, 1908

"IN 1955 there were 77,263,127 male American human beings. And every one of them . . . would have given two arms, a leg and his collection of Davy Crockett iron-ons to be Teddy Ballgame."

—BRENDAN C. BOYD AND FRED C. HARRIS ON TED WILLIAMS, THE GREAT AMERICAN BASEBALL CARD FLIPPING, TRADING AND BUBBLE GUM BOOK

"FIELDING IS AN INFINITY of possibilities, some of them seemingly impossible: the very promise of America."

—JIM KAPLAN, PLAYING THE FIELD

"BASEBALL IS STILL the national sport, having outlived Indian-killing, kept pace with war, and coexisted with football, and it will survive everything but nostalgia."

—LUKE SALISBURY, THE ANSWER IS BASEBALL

"WASHINGTON—first in war, first in peace,
last in the American League."

—CHARLES DRYDEN ON THE LOWLY SENATORS

"IF A MAN WORKED AT IT, he observed, he could make himself
do more than he thought he could do; that was baseball,
and that was America."

—TOM WICKER ON THE GRITTY DRIVE OF HALL OF FAMER ENOS
SLAUGHTER, THE ULTIMATE BASEBALL BOOK

"BASEBALL'S UNIQUE POSSESSION, the real source of our
strength, is the fan's memory of the times his daddy took
him to the game to see the great players of his youth."

—BILL VEECK, THE HUSTLER'S HANDBOOK

"NO SANITARY MEASURE that can be adopted . . . is so
calculated to induce that healthy condition of the system
which acts as a barrier to the progress of this disease
as base ball exercise each afternoon."

—BASEBALL PROMOTED AS A PREVENTATIVE FOR CHOLERA
DURING AN AMERICAN EPIDEMIC IN 1866

"Lajoie chews Red Devil tobacco. . . . Ask him if he don't."

—*Early 20th century advertisement*

"Baseball is the very symbol, the outward and visible expression of the drive and push and rush and struggle of the raging, tearing, booming nineteenth century."

—*Mark Twain, 1889*

"The idea staggered me . . . it never occurred to me that one man could start to play with the faith of fifty million people—with the single-mindedness of a burglar blowing a safe."

—*Character Nick Carraway describing the 1919 Black Sox scandal in The Great Gatsby*

"'I would like to take the great DiMaggio fishing,' the old man said. 'They say his father was a fisherman. Maybe he was as poor as we are and would understand.'"

—*Ernest Hemingway, The Old Man and the Sea*

OUR NATIONAL ANTHEM

THE HABIT OF PLAYING "The Star-Spangled Banner" before American sporting contests began with baseball during the 1918 World Series. World War I was raging in Europe, and a military order was issued that May declaring that young men not in the service find essential work in war factories or elsewhere—a law that became known as the "work or fight" rule. When Senators catcher Eddie Ainsmith appealed the loss of his draft exemption under the edict, Secretary of War Newton Baker announced July 19 that baseball was a nonessential activity—and that Ainsmith was eligible for the draft unless he quit playing and took an essential post elsewhere.

The ruling caused widespread panic among big-league owners, sure the resulting exodus to farms and factories would leave their rosters empty. Ballplayers leaving in droves left the remainder of the 1918 season in doubt, as well as the entire 1919 campaign, if the war were to continue. It was eventually decided by government officials that the regular season would conclude approximately one month early, on September 1, to be followed by the World Series. Owners, already hurt by rapidly declining attendance, championed the decision as a chance to save 30 days of salaries, and on September 5 the Cubs and Red Sox met in Chicago for the Series opener.

Boston ace Babe Ruth defeated Hippo Vaughn in Game 1, 1-0, but it was an act by Red Sox owner and musical pro-

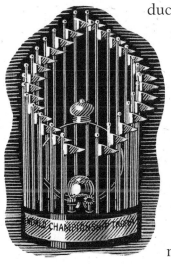

ducer Harry Frazee that had a more far-reaching impact. Frazee had hired a band to attend each Series contest, and as a tribute to enlisted players and other soldiers in Europe had it strike up a rendition of "The Star-Spangled Banner" during the seventh-inning stretch. Francis Scott Key's song had not yet become the American national anthem, but players still felt compelled to stand at attention and face the flag during the performance. Servicemen in the crowd cheered, and the crowd burst into applause at the song's conclusion.

The move was repeated each of the next two games in Chicago, and when the teams traveled to Boston for the fourth contest Frazee had the tune played before the first pitch at Fenway Park. For years afterward it would be played in Boston on special occasions, and when electric public address systems became commonplace, recordings started being heard before the start of every baseball game throughout the country. The custom passed on to other American sports and continues to this day, although Frazee is now remembered far more as the scoundrel who sold Ruth to the Yankees than as the music lover who gave the game one of its most patriotic traditions.

"Two hours is about as long as an American can wait
for the close of a baseball game—or anything else,
for that matter."

—Albert Spalding

"Both sides must understand that any blows at the thing
called baseball would be regarded by this court
as a blow to a national institution."

—Judge Kenesaw Mountain Landis, presiding over court
action between the Federal League and the Major Leagues

"Baseball is in its infancy."

—Brooklyn owner Charlie Ebbets, 1909

"He sometimes throws and catches a ball
for hours with his aide-de-camp."

—American soldier under General George Washington

"No human mind may measure the blessings conferred by
the game of Base Ball on the soldiers of the Civil War. It had
its earliest evolution when soldiers, North and South, were

striving to forget their foes by cultivating, through this grand game, fraternal friendships with comrades in arms."

—*ALBERT SPALDING, LATE 19TH CENTURY*

"GAMES PLAYED with the ball, and others of that nature, are too violent for the body and stamp no character on the mind."

—*THOMAS JEFFERSON IN A LETTER TO PETER CARR, AUGUST 19, 1785*

"I AM GLAD TO HEAR of their coming, but they will have to wait a few minutes till I get my turn at bat."

—*ABRAHAM LINCOLN, ON BEING INFORMED OF HIS NOMINATION FOR PRESIDENT, 1860*

"APRIL 21, 1863. The parade ground has been a busy place for a week or so past, ball-playing having become a mania in camp. Officers and men forget, for a time, the differences in rank and indulge in the invigorating sport with a school-boy's ardor."

—*PRIVATE ALPHERIS B. PARKER, 10TH MASSACHUSETTS, UNION ARMY*

BASEBALL, HOT DOGS, AND APPLE PIE

SINCE BABE RUTH was too young for entry into saloons, baseball has given everybody from advertisers to presidential candidates a chance to wrap themselves in the American flag. Auto makers hoping to connect their car with all things patriotic sang of "Baseball, hot dogs, apple pie, and Chevrolet," while for nearly a century the most American of holidays—the Fourth of July and Labor Day—always meant doubleheaders (and often fireworks) at ballparks large and small.

Even every president but Rutherford B. Hayes has been linked in some way to the game. George Washington tossed a ball with an aide at Valley Forge, George Bush captained his Yale team and was in uniform for a visit from Babe Ruth (a picture often seen during the '88 campaign), and sports cable-television channel ESPN debuted its 1996 baseball commercials with a tall, top-hatted gent by the name of Lincoln serving as its spokesman.

"SUDDENLY THERE CAME a scattering of fire of which the three outfielders caught the brunt; the center field was hit and was captured, the left and right field managed to get back into our lines. The attack . . . was repelled without serious difficulty, but we had lost not only our center field, but . . . the only baseball in Alexandria, Texas."

—GEORGE PUTNAM, UNION ARMY

"[BASEBALL SWEPT] like dysentery through the Army camps, down the South Atlantic coast, and out into the Midwest . . . by the time the nation's wounds were bandaged . . . [it had become] the most popular game in the land."

—TRISTRAM POTTER COFFIN

"NEXT TO ABRAHAM LINCOLN and George Washington, the name of A.G. Spalding is the most famous in American literature."

—BOSTON HERALD EDITORIAL, AROUND 1880

"GOOD BALLPLAYERS make good citizens."

—CHESTER ARTHUR

"WITH ALL OF HIS LOVE of outdoor life and sports, Mr. [Theodore] Roosevelt did not go within the ball grounds during his seven years in the White House."

—THE WASHINGTON POST, *APRIL 20, 1909*

"I LIKE TO SEE Quentin practicing baseball. It gives me hope that one of my boys will not take after his father in this respect, and will prove able to play the national game."

—*THEODORE ROOSEVELT*

"WE OWE A GREAT DEAL to Base Ball. . . . It is one of the reasons why American soldiers are the best in the world— quick witted, swift to act, ready of judgment, capable of going into action without officers. . . . It is one of the reasons why as a nation we impress visitors as quick, alert, confident and trained for independent action."

—CHICAGO AMERICAN, *1906*

". . . THE EXPONENT of American Courage, Confidence, Combatism; American Dash, Discipline, Determinism; American Energy, Eagerness, Enthusiasm; American Pluck,

Persistency, Performance; American Spirit, Sagacity, Success; American Vim, Vigor, Virility. . . ."

—A PORTION OF ALBERT SPALDING'S 1911 ANALYSIS DECLARING BASEBALL AS "AMERICA'S GAME"

"**A** BIG ENOUGH BOY to enjoy the national game—and a man big enough to guide our country through its greatest crisis."

—WORDS ACCOMPANYING PICTURE OF PRESIDENT WOODROW WILSON THROWING OUT THE FIRST BALL OF THE SEASON, COVER OF 1917 WORLD SERIES PROGRAM

"**B**ASE BALL RECEIVED a knockout wallop yesterday when Secretary Baker ruled . . . players in the draft age must obtain employment calculated to aid in the successful prosecution of the war or shoulder guns and fight."

—FROM THE WASHINGTON STAR, JULY 21, 1918

"**T**HE GAME OF BASEBALL is a clean, straight game, and it summons to its presence everybody who enjoys clean, straight athletics. It furnishes amusement to the thousands and thousands."

—WILLIAM HOWARD TAFT

WARTIME BASEBALL

NEVER DID BASEBALL take on as much patriotic significance as during World War II. Some ballplayers had been drafted after the war broke out in Europe late in 1939, but it wasn't until the attack on Pearl Harbor following the 1941 season that those in the game became fully immersed in the cause. Detroit Tigers slugger Hank Greenberg, who had just finished a year in the Army, re-enlisted the day after Pearl Harbor—and other players including fireballer Bob Feller soon followed suit. The near-record attendance and titanic feats of the previous season—most notably Joe DiMaggio's 56-game hitting steak and Ted Williams's .406 average—were quickly forgotten, and as the U.S. suffered early setbacks in the Pacific, the same question posed in 1918 arose again: Could baseball survive?

A solid supporter of the game (if not as rabid a fan as Woodrow Wilson), President Franklin Delano Roosevelt understood the essential place baseball held in American life. Their loved ones fighting and dying abroad, their everyday existence altered by circum-stances such as the introduc-tion of food and gasoline rations, and their peace of mind threatened by the peril that war would come to U.S. soil, citizens clung to whatever

pieces of normalcy they could—especially that which could help them momentarily escape from the daily headlines and casualty lists. Writing to Commissioner Kenesaw Mountain Landis in what became known as the "green light" letter, President Roosevelt spelled out that although ballplayers would face the same military obligations as other citizens, baseball would continue in 1942.

Despite the loss of Greenberg, Feller, and other stars, enough luminaries remained for the '42 season to be virtually unchanged from the previous year in terms of player skill. By the following spring, however, so many top-notch and even everyday players had departed that rosters began to resemble a Who's Who of old-timers clinging on, unseasoned youngsters learning on the job, and others who stood no chance at making the big leagues under normal circumstances. Perhaps the most prominent examples of the era were 15-year-old Reds pitcher Joe Nuxhall and Browns outfielder Pete Gray—who was an inspiration to countless injured vets in playing 77 games of the 1945 season with one arm. The game's image, however, was never more patriotic. Relay races and other pregame events were staged with the proceeds all going to war bonds, radio broadcasts of World Series contests were sent to troops over Armed Forces Radio, and the story went that Japanese soldiers wishing to harass their U.S. counterparts would go screaming into battle with the cry: "The hell with Babe Ruth!"

"BASEBALL IS OUR national game."

—CALVIN COOLIDGE

"BY BRINGING the baseball pennant to Washington, you have made the National Capital more truly the center of worthy and honorable national aspirations."

—CALVIN COOLIDGE, ADDRESSING MEMBERS OF THE AMERICAN LEAGUE CHAMPION WASHINGTON SENATORS

"NEXT TO RELIGION, baseball has furnished a greater impact on American life than any other institution."

—HERBERT HOOVER

"I KNOW, but I had a better year than Hoover."

—BABE RUTH'S RESPONSE WHEN A REPORTER POINTED OUT HIS 1930 SALARY DEMAND OF $80,000 TOPPED THAT OF THE PRESIDENT'S $75,000 SALARY

"WHAT DOES BASEBALL DO for America? It provides an opportunity for hundreds of thousands of war workers to relax in the fresh air and sunshine—and to continue to

enjoy something that has been a significant part of American life for almost 100 years."

—Representative La Vern Dilweg, Wisconsin, in a speech to the U.S. House of Representatives on why baseball should continue during World War II

"I honestly feel that it would be best for the country to keep baseball going . . . if 300 teams use 5,000 or 6,000 players, these players are a definite recreational asset to at least 20,000,000 of their fellow citizens—and that in my judgment is thoroughly worthwhile."

Franklin Delano Roosevelt's "green light" letter to Judge Kenesaw Mountain Landis, January 15, 1942

"May the sun never set on American baseball."

—Harry Truman, marking the 75th anniversary of the major leagues, February 2, 1951

"Last year, more Americans went to symphonies than went to baseball games. This may be viewed as an alarming statistic, but I think that both baseball and the country will endure."

—John F. Kennedy

THE SAGA OF SATCHEL PAIGE

"GO VERY LIGHT on the vices, such as carrying on in society. The social ramble ain't restful." Such was the teaching of Satchel Paige, part pitcher, part philosopher, and full-time raconteur. Satch likely told more tales and accomplished more actual feats than any man in baseball history next to Babe Ruth. And Satch did so while spending most of his career denied the opportunity to play in the major leagues. Slugging catcher Josh Gibson earned the nickname "the Black Babe Ruth," but a more appropriate choice for that title would have been Paige, a beanpole-tall, gangly road warrior who, over some 40-odd years of pitching wherever allowed, made people laugh and did more to break down baseball's racial barriers than anyone else.

The actual number of games Paige won while barnstorming through small towns and big cities over the decades will never be known, nor is it important; what he gave the game above shutouts or strikeouts was an unflappable ability to perform on command. He could call in his outfielders and strike out the side, throw a ball directly over a cigarette on four of five attempts, and deliver pitches from a variety of angles with results both comical and efficient. White major-leaguers routinely said he was the best hurler they had ever faced, but Satch did not put up a public stink about waiting until he was a reported 42 years old to reach the bigs. Even then he knew where he stood, as evidenced from his words upon being inducted into the Hall of Fame: "The only change is that baseball has turned Paige from a second-class citizen into a second-class immortal."

"Mr. Spritzer, you spoke earlier of 'Yankee Ingenuity.' According to the information I have just received, you should have spoken of 'Pirate Ingenuity.'"

—Chief Justice of the Supreme Court Earl Warren to Ralph S. Spritzer, assistant to the Solicitor General, upon finding out that the Pirates had topped the Yankees in the World Series on Bill Mazeroski's homer, October 13, 1960

"A couple of years ago, they told me I was too young to be president and you were too old to be playing baseball. But we fooled them."

—45-year-old John F. Kennedy to 41-year-old Stan Musial at the 1962 All-Star Game

"WE CHEER FOR THE SENATORS, we pray for the Senators, and we hope that the Supreme Court does not declare that unconstitutional."

—*LYNDON JOHNSON, JULY 10, 1962*

"I DON'T KNOW a lot about politics, but I know a lot about baseball."

—*RICHARD NIXON, 1981*

"THE WIRE has gone dead."

—*NOTE FROM THE WIRELESS OPERATOR TO RONALD REAGAN WHEN HE WAS A RADIO SPORTS BROADCASTER IN THE MID-1930S; REAGAN MADE UP PITCHES FOR OVER SIX MINUTES UNTIL THE CONNECTION WAS RESTORED*

"NOSTALGIA BUBBLES within me, and I might have to be dragged away."

—*RONALD REAGAN, HOSTING A LUNCHEON FOR 32 HALL OF FAMERS AT THE WHITE HOUSE, MARCH 27, 1981*

"THIS IS REALLY more fun than being president. I really do love baseball and I wish we could do this out on the lawn every day."

—RONALD REAGAN ON PLAYING BALL WITH OLD-TIMERS DURING NATIONAL BASEBALL MONTH, 1983

"BASEBALL IS JUST the great American pastime. I think it's the joy of feeling part of [the game] more than other sports."

—GEORGE BUSH, THE WASHINGTON POST, MARCH 31, 1989

"NOLAN SAYS THROW IT high because amateurs get out there, no matter how good they are, and throw it in the dirt. You get more of an 'ooooh' [from the crowd] if you heave it over the [catcher's] head instead of going with the fast-breaking deuce into the dirt."

—GEORGE BUSH ON ADVICE NOLAN RYAN GAVE HIM ON THROWING OUT THE FIRST BALL WHILE PRESIDENT

THE GLORIFICATION OF BASEBALL

WITH THE NOTABLE EXCEPTIONS of war and romance, baseball seems to have been glorified in film, television, books, and song more than any other American pastime. The highs and lows of life as defined in a single at bat moved masses in the celebrated Ernest Lawrence Thayer poem, "Casey at the Bat," and while the line "there is no joy in Mudville" has become a familiar way of describing failure, hordes of fans have seen fit to rewrite the ending so the hero not strike out. The song "Take Me Out to the Ballgame" has been subject to more renditions and revisions than anything this side of "Happy Birthday," while millions of folks who don't know one double-play combo from another know the rhythmic flow of the words "Tinker to Evers to Chance."

When Simon and Garfunkel sought to capture the lost innocence of Vietnam-era Americans, all it took was one line in their 1967 hit "Mrs. Robinson": "Where have you gone, Joe DiMaggio? Our nation turns its lonely eyes to you." Beginning with Thomas Edison's 1898 glimpse of two amateur clubs battling it out in "The Ball Game," baseball has been the subject of hundreds of screen adaptations. If not always great art, the results are at least resoundingly American—leaving fans to hope that fathers and sons will play catch, just like Kevin Costner and his dad did in *Field of Dreams*.

"I ALWAYS TURN to the sports section first. The sports section records people's accomplishments; the front page nothing but man's failures."

—*EARL WARREN*

"BASEBALL'S STATUS in the life of the nation is so pervasive that it would not strain credulity to say the Court can take judicial notice that baseball is everybody's business. The game is on a higher ground; it behooves everyone to keep it there."

—*JUDGE I.B. COOPER, IN THE CASE OF FLOOD V. KUHN IN WHICH CURT FLOOD CHALLENGED BASEBALL'S RESERVE CLAUSE*

"WHAT DO YOU IMAGINE the American people would think of me if I wasted my time going to the ball game?"

—*GROVER CLEVELAND TO CAP ANSON, DURING A VISIT OF THE CHICAGO WHITE STOCKINGS TO THE WHITE HOUSE, 1885*

HORSEHIDE SENSE

"YOU DON'T SAVE A PITCHER for tomorrow. Tomorrow it might rain."

—LEO DUROCHER

BIRDIE'S TWO LETTERS

THE JOB OF A BASEBALL MANAGER is packed with pressure. Questions of who and how to pitch, hit, and position players come up repeatedly. Following every contest there are hordes of radio, television, and print reporters demanding reasons for the decisions just made. Since the 25 ballplayers under a manager's tutelage all desire to play every day, the soothing of egos is yet another task. If a team begins floundering, the manager is usually the first to lose his job.

All this can get to be too much, but Milwaukee Braves manager Birdie Tebbetts devised a surefire way for dealing with the stress that he passed on to his successor, Bobby Bragan, in 1963. Bragan found two envelopes in his desk drawer marked "No. 1" and "No. 2," along with the simple instructions: "Open in emergency only." The season got underway, and with the Braves struggling and his solutions exhausted, Bragan turned to the drawer and opened envelope No. 1. "Blame it on me," the message inside read. When Milwaukee improved only slightly during the 1964 season, Bragan looked again for solace inside envelope No. 2. Perhaps there would be some words of wisdom Tebbetts had to offer, or a new way of aligning the club that could spark a winning streak. The message this time turned out to be a task for Bragan: "Prepare two letters."

"KEEP YOUR EYE CLEAR and hit 'em where they ain't."

—WEE WILLIE KEELER

"YOU CAN LEARN little from victory.
You can learn everything from defeat."

—CHRISTY MATHEWSON

"GOODBYE, BOYS, I am done with this kind of living."

—BILLY SUNDAY UPON QUITTING BASEBALL TO GO INTO PREACHING

"EVERY GREAT BATTER works on the theory that the pitcher is
more afraid of him than he is of the pitcher."

—TY COBB, THE TIGER WORE SPIKES

"I WAS NOT ABLE to understand how it could be right to pay
an actor, or a singer, or an instrumentalist for entertaining
the public, and wrong to pay a ball player for doing
exactly the same thing."

—ALBERT SPALDING, AROUND 1900

THE FIRST TOOLS OF IGNORANCE

MAJOR-LEAGUERS ONLY BEGAN WEARING batting helmets on a regular basis in the mid-1950s, but more incredible is that there was once a time when even catchers wore no protective equipment of any kind. It wasn't until well into the game's third modern decade that Harvard University coach and player Fred Winthrop Thayer invented a padded metal grate that Crimson catcher James Tyng wore over his face for Harvard's April 12, 1877, game against a semipro Massachusetts opponent. It both protected Tyng from injury and enabled him to move closer to the plate—an advantage to his pitcher and a disadvantage to baserunners. The device actually received criticism from some as unbefitting the rugged nature of the sport, but enough receivers wanted one that Thayer was granted a patent the following year. Still, it wasn't until 30 years later that New York Giants star Roger Bresnahan brought the mask (along with his own invention, shin guards) into the majors.

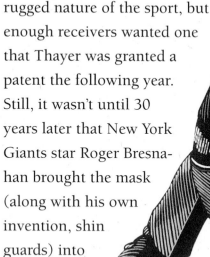

"DON'T LOOK BACK. Something might be gaining on you."

—SATCHEL PAIGE

"THE SECRET OF MY SUCCESS was clean living
and a fast-moving outfield."

—PITCHER LEFTY GOMEZ

"DON'T QUIT until every base is uphill."

—BABE RUTH, THE BABE RUTH STORY

"MOST IMPORTANT OF ALL—and this goes not alone for
baseball but every other profession—save your money!
If I had saved from the start of my career, I might have
had a million dollars today."

—BABE RUTH, BABE RUTH'S OWN BOOK FOR BASEBALL

"KEEP it low."

—TIGER CATCHER BOB SWIFT, GIVING LES CAIN ADVICE ON HOW TO
PITCH TO 3'7" BROWNS BATTER EDDIE GAEDEL, RAIN DELAYS

CANDY AND THE CURVEBALL

ONE GREAT CONTROVERSY looming in the early days of baseball was the debate over whether or not a pitcher could
actually make a ball curve. Early major-league rules dictated
that a pitcher keep his arm below his belt at all times; and
without the benefit of a full windup, any tricks were useful
in a hurler's attempt to gain speed and deception over batters. At 5′9″, 120 pounds, William Arthur "Candy" Cummings rang up an impressive amateur record despite his
size—which he
attributed to
his ability to
throw the
first actual
curveball.
Claiming
he initially
devised the
idea of twist-
ing pitches at age

14 in 1863 by watching the path clam shells took as he
tossed them at the beach, Candy's trick was snapping his
wrist as he released the ball—a method that once earned
him a broken wrist but enough of a legend to get him into
the Hall of Fame despite a six-year career in the majors.

"BASEBALL IS ONLY a game, but they keep a book on you. When it's all over for you, the game has got you measured."

—JOE GARAGIOLA, BASEBALL IS A FUNNY GAME

"IN BASEBALL you're with every guy on your club and you're against every player on the other club from the time the game starts until it's over. You've got your whole club with you, too, but you're all alone sometimes where they can't help you."

—JOE GARAGIOLA, BASEBALL IS A FUNNY GAME

"IN BASEBALL, you don't know nothing."

—YOGI BERRA, BASEBALL: AN ILLUSTRATED HISTORY

"YOU CAN SEE a lot just by observing."

—YOGI BERRA

"BASEBALL IS 90 PERCENT mental; the other half is physical."

—YOGI BERRA

"I HIT WITH A BAT, not with my face."

—*YOGI BERRA, RESPONDING TO NEEDLES*
ABOUT HIS HOMELY COMPLEXION

"I WANT TO THANK everyone who made this day necessary."

—*YOGI BERRA, ADDRESSING THE ST. LOUIS CROWD*
ON YOGI BERRA APPRECIATION DAY

"THIS SHOULD PROVE the leather is mightier than the wood."

—*WHITE SOX MANAGER FIELDER ALLISON JONES AFTER HIS 1906*
"HITLESS WONDERS" WON THE WORLD SERIES WITH A
.228 CLUB BATTING AVERAGE

"NO TWO PITCHES throughout the entire nine innings
[should] come up to the plate at the same speed. . . . Don't
let the batter get stepping in time with your rate of speed.
If they step with your pitch, they can hit
the fastest thing you throw."

—*HALL OF FAME PITCHER GROVER CLEVELAND ALEXANDER,*
AROUND 1920

"I FIGURED IF I WASN'T a good ballplayer, it wouldn't make any difference where I played; but if I was a good ballplayer, then I wanted to be with the Yankees."

—*TOMMY HENRICH, BASEBALL BETWEEN THE LINES*

"YOU GOTTA BE A MAN to play baseball for a living, but you gotta have a lot of little boy in you, too."

—*ROY CAMPANELLA*

"I LEARNED A LONG TIME AGO you're wasting your time trying to make a player use his head."

—*REDS MANAGER PAT MORAN*

"GIMME GOOD PITCHING and long hitting, and let the rest of them managers get just as smart as they want!"

—*MANAGER WILBERT ROBINSON*

"HITTING IS timing. Pitching is upsetting timing."

—*WARREN SPAHN*

GAMBLIN' LOU PINIELLA

OUTFIELDER LOU PINIELLA WAS KNOWN as a "gambler." He
was the type of player who often depended purely on
instincts to guide his on-field decisions. On October 2,
1978, Piniella's good sense meant the difference in a winner-
take-all American League East playoff game between the
Yankees and Red Sox at Fen-
way Park. New York had
24-game winner Ron
Guidry pitching, but the
Sox took a 2-0 lead into the
sixth inning and looked
ready to break things open.
Fred Lynn came up with two on
and two out and pulled a line
drive toward the right-field corner. The midafternoon sun
blinding him terribly, Piniella had no idea where the ball
was. Running to where he felt it would land, he wound up
hunched over but in perfect position to make the catch and
keep the game close.

After the Yankees rallied to take a 5-4 lead into the
ninth, Boston had speedy Rick Burleson at first with one
out when Jerry Remy hit another smash toward Piniella.
The sun was even worse now, but knowing Burleson would
be watching him, Lou pounded his glove as if he was going
to make an easy catch—again moving where he thought the
ball would land. He didn't catch this one, but Remy's hit

took one bounce and went directly into Piniella's lunging glove. An amazed Burleson could advance only to second, and Jim Rice followed with a deep fly ball that would have tied the game had a runner been on third. Carl Yastrzemski popped out, New York won 5-4, and two weeks later the Yanks were world champions—thanks in large part to the gambler.

"WHY NOT HAVE some fun today? Don't try to throw so hard and use more curves and change-ups."

—DODGER CATCHER NORM SHERRY TO SANDY KOUFAX, SPRING TRAINING 1961; KOUFAX WAS 36-40 LIFETIME BEFORE THE SUGGESTION AND 129-47 AFTER

"YOU SPEND A GOOD PIECE of your life gripping a baseball and in the end it turns out that it was the other way around all the time."

—JIM BOUTON, BALL FOUR

"YOU'RE ONLY as smart as your ERA."

—JIM BOUTON, I'M GLAD YOU DIDN'T TAKE IT PERSONALLY

". . . SOMETIMES IN THIS GAME it's as good to be lucky as it is to be good."

—*VIDA BLUE, VIDA: HIS OWN STORY*

"I'D WALK me."

—*WILLIE MCCOVEY ON HOW HE WOULD PITCH TO HIMSELF, BASEBALL DIGEST, SEPTEMBER 1971*

"GUESSING WHAT THE PITCHER is going to throw is 80 percent of being a successful hitter. The other 20 percent is just execution."

—*HANK AARON, HANK AARON . . . 714 AND BEYOND*

"WHEN YOU'RE 21, you're a prospect. When you're 30, you're a suspect."

—*WHITE SOX PITCHER JIM MCGLOTHLIN*

"THE ONLY THING that's certain is they'll play the National Anthem before every game."

—*RICK MONDAY, BASEBALL QUOTATIONS*

". . . YOU SAY MICKEY MANTLE, I'll say Willie Mays; if you say Henry Aaron, I'll say Roberto Clemente. When you're competing at that level of ability, the margins of difference aren't that great."

—TOM SEAVER, THE GREATEST TEAM OF ALL TIME

"PEOPLE ASK ME how I'd like to be remembered. I tell them I'd like to be remembered as the guy who hit the line drive over Bobby Richardson's head."

—WILLIE McCOVEY, WHO ENDED THE SEVENTH GAME OF THE 1962 WORLD SERIES WITH A VICIOUS LINER CAUGHT BY YANKEE SECOND BASEMAN RICHARDSON WITH RUNNERS AT SECOND AND THIRD IN A 2-1 NEW YORK WIN, BASEBALL ANECDOTES

"IF YOU HAVE TO begin fining them, it's time to get rid of them."

—HUGHIE JENNINGS'S MANAGERIAL THEORY

"WELL, YOU CAN'T win them all."

—CONNIE MACK ON HIS 1916 A'S, WHO WENT 36-117

MERKLE'S BONER

A CUNNING ACT OF BASEBALL knowledge helped one man's team to a championship while condemning another to the history books as perpetrator of a blunder so disastrous that the term "bonehead" is listed under his photograph in some baseball reference books. On September 23, 1908, the New York Giants and Chicago Cubs met in a crucial game at the Polo Grounds in which the winner would take first place in the National League in the waning days of the season. The score was tied 1-1 in the last of the ninth, with two outs and runners on first and third for the Giants. A single to center brought the man in from third with what appeared to be the winning run, while the runner on first—Fred Merkle— stopped short in his path toward second base and headed toward the Giants clubhouse.

Merkle's trip, however, was a bit premature. The official rules state that no run can score with two outs until a possible force play has been completed, meaning the play on which the game-winner scored would not be complete until Merkle touched second base ahead of the ball. It is unlikely many in the park were even paying attention to Merkle or the ball at this point, but one of those who was happened to also know the rule—Cubs second baseman Johnny Evers. Even as Giants players and fans stormed the field in jubilation, Evers motioned for center fielder Solly Hofman to throw him the ball so he could tag second and nullify the run. Disputing accounts claim either an unruly fan intercepted Hofman's throw or Giants third base coach Joe McGinnity (fighting off Cubs shortstop Joe Tinker) grabbed it on an overthrow; in either case the ball apparently wound up being tossed into the stands.

As his teammates began pushing Merkle back toward second base, either a fan threw the original ball back to Evers from the stands or a second ball somehow appeared. It was tossed to Evers. In any case, umpire Hank O'Day—who had seen Evers make a similar claim against Pittsburgh days earlier—called Merkle out and stopped play amidst the chaos. While New York papers later hit the streets claiming the Giants victors, National League President Harry Pullman declared the contest a tie to be replayed following the end of the season. As luck would have it, the two clubs were also tied in the standings when the campaign concluded, and Chicago won the rematch 4-2 for the pennant. The play became known as the "Merkle Boner," the first time that word would be used to symbolize a dumb play.

"SHOW me a good loser, and I'll show you an idiot."

— LEO DUROCHER

"IF YOU'RE IN PROFESSIONAL SPORTS, buddy, and you don't care whether you win or lose, you are going to finish last. Because that's where those guys finish, they finish last."

—*LEO DUROCHER, NICE GUYS FINISH LAST*

"I BELIEVE IN RULES. I also believe I have a right to test the rules by seeing how far they can be bent."

—*LEO DUROCHER, NICE GUYS FINISH LAST*

"THERE ARE FIVE THINGS you can do in baseball—run, throw, catch, hit, and hit with power."

—*LEO DUROCHER*

"MANAGING IS NEVER FUN. If you pull off something big, it's expected. If you fail, you're a bum."

—*SKIPPER PAUL RICHARDS, BASEBALL'S GREATEST MANAGERS*

"IT AIN'T OVER till it's over."

—*YOGI BERRA*

"JUST HANG THE NATIONAL LEAGUE schedule on my tombstone each year. Then, after people are through visiting their loved ones in the cemetery, they can come by my grave and see if the Dodgers are playing home or away that night."

—*DODGERS MINOR-LEAGUE MANAGER TOMMY LASORDA, TELLING CLUB PRESIDENT WALTER O'MALLEY HOW HE COULD KEEP WORKING FOR THE ORGANIZATION AFTER HIS DEATH,* BASEBALL DIGEST, *FEBRUARY 1996*

"JUST GIVE ME a happy ballclub, and we'll be hard to beat."

—*BILLY SOUTHWORTH,* BASEBALL'S GREATEST MANAGERS

"IF I HAD ONE WISH in the world today, it would be that Jackie Robinson could be here to see this happen."

—*FRANK ROBINSON ON BEING MADE THE FIRST BLACK MANAGER IN MAJOR-LEAGUE HISTORY*

"BASEBALL IS PITCHING, fundamentals, and three-run homers."

—*EARL WEAVER,* HOW LIFE IMITATES THE WORLD SERIES

THE MIRACLE BRAVES

THE 1913 BOSTON BRAVES PLACED FIFTH in the National League with a 69-82 record, not very impressive but a big improvement from their 52-101, last-place showing of the previous year and their highest finish in 11 summers. The difference, most agreed, was their new manager—George Tweedy Stallings. He was a former bush-league catcher who possessed a keen mind for the game and an affinity for scrappy, hustling players in his own image. Stallings knew how to pump up his troops with confidence, but could also cut down a boneheaded performer with the best of them. His players, who respected him immensely, would usually join in the cursing of their teammate from the dugout.

Stallings called his strategy "playing the percentages," and he held tactical meetings with his team on a daily basis. When it came time to put his 1914 club together, he acquired the services of former Cubs second baseman Johnny Evers, whose own sharp instincts had helped Chicago win a pennant on the famous "Merkle Boner" two years before. One writer said that "if George Stallings was the Eisenhower of the 1914 Braves, his Patton was Johnny Evers."

Even this combination could not keep the ragtag club from starting the season 4-18 and dropping into last place. Stallings never panicked, and Evers never let his teammates lose hope, but with the exception of one day in June the club remained in the cellar until July 18. Nobody seemed to notice the Braves had played well over .500 since their awful start—or that they were hungry for more.

Suddenly, everything started to click. Stallings settled on a three-man pitching rotation of Dick Rudolph, Lefty Tyler, and Bill James, and the trio repaid their skipper's faith with 69 victories between them—most coming after July 4. Evers and shortstop Walter "Rabbit" Maranville turned in spectacular plays, Hank Gowdy steadied at catcher, and Stallings juggled six outfielders in and out of the lineup guided by the belief (not as yet popularized) that left-handed batters should face right-handed pitchers and vice versa. On August 23, following a wild five-week ride up the standings, Boston tied the Giants for first place. The next week, after beating New York in a big Labor Day series at Fenway Park, the Braves were in first alone—where they would remain.

Stallings's troops won 52 of 66 in their hot stretch, recorded 18 shutouts after July 4, and won the pennant by $10\frac{1}{2}$ games with the benefit of just three reliable pitchers and one .300 hitter. A World Series sweep of Connie Mack's heavily favored Athletics clinched Boston's spot in history as the "Miracle Braves," and Stallings as baseball's "Miracle Man."

"THROW STRIKES. The plate don't move."

—*SATCHEL PAIGE, STRIKEOUT: A CELEBRATION OF THE ART OF PITCHING*

"PROFESSIONAL CLUBS, to keep in existence, must have gate money; to receive gate money, they must play games; and to enable them to play games, their opponents must have faith that such games will prove remunerative."

—*EXCERPT OF LETTER FROM BOSTON MANAGER HARRY WRIGHT OF THE AMERICAN ASSOCIATION TO WILLIAM HULBERT, BACKING HIS PLAN TO FORM A NEW "NATIONAL LEAGUE," 1875*

"THE TRADITION of professional baseball always has been agreeably free of chivalry. The rule is: Do anything you can get away with."

—*HEYWOOD BROUN, WRITING ON THE GAME AT THE TURN OF THE CENTURY*

"ONLY IN BASEBALL can a team player be a pure individualist first and a team player second, within the rules and the spirit of the game."

—*BRANCH RICKEY, THE AMERICAN DIAMOND*

"I HAVE ALWAYS MAINTAINED that the best remedy for a batting slump is two wads of cotton. One for each ear."

—BILL VEECK, THE HUSTLER'S HANDBOOK

"I BECAME A MAJOR-LEAGUE manager in several cities and was discharged. We call it discharged because there was no question I had to leave."

—CASEY STENGEL

"BASEBALL IS THE MOST INTELLECTUAL game because most of the action goes on in your head."

—HENRY KISSINGER

"I BET YOU WISH Drysdale was Jewish, too."

—LEFTY GOMEZ TO DODGER MANAGER WALTER ALSTON, AFTER ALSTON'S STARTER DON DRYSDALE HAD BEEN SHELLED IN THE FIRST GAME OF THE 1965 WORLD SERIES WHILE SUBBING FOR SANDY KOUFAX—WHO REFUSED TO PLAY ON YOM KIPPUR, THE ULTIMATE BASEBALL BOOK

STENGEL'S REVIVAL

THE MOST FAMOUS MANAGER of his and all time might have
been viewed by history as no more than a clown were it not
for a nifty piece of timing. A colorful, scrappy outfielder
during his playing career with five teams, Casey Stengel hit
.393 in three World Series but was best remembered for
stepping to the plate in Brooklyn, tipping his cap to a
jeering crowd, and having a bird fly out. As manager of
awful Dodgers and Boston Braves teams, he finished seventh five times in nine seasons and kept players amused
with such comments as: "I'm not
complaining about losing.
But, gee, couldn't you
take a little longer
doin' it?" When he
was hit by a cab and
forced to the sidelines with
a broken leg, one sports writer
suggested the cabbie be heralded as
"the man who has done the most for
Boston baseball in 1943." By '44 Stengel was skippering in
the minors, presumably to stay.

Then fate stepped in. Yankees general manager George
Weiss was looking for a new field boss after firing Bucky
Harris, and remembered Casey fondly from when Stengel
had managed for him in minor-league Oakland. Weiss
brought Stengel aboard—much to the amazement of fans

and writers who knew his clownish image—and Casey proceeded to win World Series championships his first five years helped by a roster peppered with All-Stars and Hall of Famers. Eventually he won 10 pennants in 12 years, and when he said after one championship that "I couldn't have done it without my players," he was only half-joking. He had already tried doing it without them, and it hadn't worked.

"SPEED IS A DECIDEDLY BAD qualification for pitching unless accuracy goes with it."

—CY YOUNG, STRIKEOUT: A CELEBRATION OF
THE ART OF PITCHING

"I DON'T RATE 'EM, I just catch 'em."

—WILLIE MAYS, WHEN ASKED IF HE HAD A FAVORITE AMONG HIS
DEFENSIVE GEMS, THE BASEBALL LIFE OF WILLIE MAYS

"IF YOU'RE NOT HAVING FUN [in baseball], you miss the point of everything."

—CHRIS CHAMBLISS

BIG-LEAGUE HEROES

"THERE IS ALWAYS some kid who may be
seeing me for the first or last time.
I owe him my best."

—*JOE DIMAGGIO*

BREAKING DOWN THE BARRIER

SINCE THE OWNERS drove Fleet Walker from the Toledo squad in 1884, more than 60 years passed without another black player taking a spot on a major-league roster. African Americans formed the Negro Leagues, but an unwritten "understanding" amongst the old guard of big-league owners kept such stars from ever playing alongside the Ruths and Gehrigs.

By the late 1930s, however, black newspapers and the occasional white columnist had taken up the cause to break down baseball's color barrier. Hard facts backed up their pleas. Black All-Star teams more than held their own in postseason barnstorming series with major-league outfits, and Negro League games often drew huge crowds to big-league ballparks. The winds of change appeared to be coming, but officials at all levels of white baseball—led by Commissioner Kenesaw Mountain Landis—refused to act. Only in the fall of 1945, when Brooklyn Dodgers President Branch Rickey signed Negro Leaguer Jackie Robinson to a minor-league contract, was someone sensible enough to challenge the status quo.

A former four-sport star at UCLA, Robinson was a great athlete and fine second baseman—but not the most likely choice to be torchbearer. Other Negro Leaguers such as Josh Gibson and Monte Irvin were bigger stars, but Rickey made his move with more than baseball talent in mind. As an army lieutenant, Robinson had nearly been court-martialed for refusing to move to the back of a military bus, and he possessed the fierce pride and self-determination Rickey knew would be needed to withstand the verbal and physical abuse that would come his way. "Do you want a ballplayer who's afraid to fight back?" Robinson reportedly asked in their first meeting. "No," Rickey responded. "I want a player with guts enough *not* to fight back."

After one outstanding minor-league season in Montreal, Robinson joined the Dodgers in the spring of 1947. He was subjected to countless beanballs at the plate and spikings from opponents as a second baseman, and many players wished him out of the majors. Displaying the class and courage (and keeping his word to Rickey) to neither acknowledge nor be intimidated by these challenges, Robinson also proved an exceptional player in leading the Dodgers to the 1947 pennant—their first of six during his decade with the club. By 1949, Robinson had been named the National League Most Valuable Player, the color line was gone for good, and the major leagues could finally be considered the showplace for all of baseball's best talent.

THE BROOKLYN GIANT

IF A MAN IS MEASURED by his reaction to challenges, Hall of Fame catcher Roy Campanella should be remembered as a giant more than a Dodger. A member of the Negro National League by the age of 15, he had to wait 10 seasons for the major-league doors to swing open to blacks. Eventually signed by Dodger President Branch Rickey, "Campy" joined fellow trailblazer Jackie Robinson in Brooklyn in 1948 and became an anchor on five pennant-winning teams. Campanella was an MVP in 1951, 1953, and '55. He was a clubhouse leader with his brilliant grin and infectious enthusiasm. His career snuffed out at age 36 by a 1958 car accident that left him a quadriplegic, Campy never let a wheelchair dampen his zest for living. And in four ensuing decades as a Dodger instructor, coach, and community-relations man, he touched more lives than he ever could have with a few more home runs.

"OUR BOYS DID NOBLY, but fortune was against us. Though defeated, not disgraced."

—PART OF A WIRE SENT BY CINCINNATI RED STOCKINGS PRESIDENT AARON B. CHAMPION AFTER HIS TEAM'S FIRST LOSS IN OVER 80 GAMES, JUNE 14, 1870

"EVERY MAGNATE in the country is indebted to this man for the establishment of baseball as a business, and every patron for furnishing him with a systematic recreation. Every player is indebted to him for inaugurating an occupation by which he gains a livelihood, and the country at large for adding one more industry to furnish employment."

—THE SPORTING LIFE ON HARRY WRIGHT, AROUND 1870

"IT IS NOT SO DIGNIFIED as some of the learned professions, but I would rather be a good baseball player and win the pennant for my club than be a poor, dishonest merchant, constantly failing and swindling my creditors, or a briefless lawyer hunting up divorce scandals for a livelihood."

—REV. THOMAS E. GREEN, OCTOBER 4, 1885, AS QUOTED IN THE SPORTING NEWS, SEPTEMBER 26, 1967

"HIS FACE IS THAT of a Greek hero, his manner that of a Church of England Bishop, and he is the father of the greatest sport the world has ever known."

—THE NEW YORK TIMES ON AL SPALDING, 1899

"To protect and benefit ourselves collectively and individually. To promote a high standard of professional conduct. To foster and encourage the interests of . . . Base Ball."

—*Preamble for The Brotherhood of Professional Base Ball Players, 1885*

"The game of baseball is a clean, straight game, and it summons to its presence everybody who enjoys clean, straight athletics. It furnishes amusement to the thousands and thousands."

—*President William Howard Taft, The Sporting News, May 4, 1910*

"It's great to be young and a Giant."

—*New York Giants second baseman Larry Doyle*

"You have one of the greatest teams I've ever seen. I have a great team, too, but you beat us."

—*John McGraw to Connie Mack following the 1911 World Series*

"WHY SHOULD I let it ruin my life? I had a wife and two children, and they had to eat."

—CARL MAYS, EXPLAINING WHY HE CONTINUED PITCHING IN 1920 AFTER ONE OF HIS THROWS KILLED CLEVELAND'S RAY CHAPMAN

". . . THERE WAS SOMETHING about the two of us, in the same park on the same day, battling it out, that made it a great afternoon, even if I had to lose."

—HEINIE MANUSH ON HIS RACE FOR THE 1926 AMERICAN LEAGUE BATTING TITLE AGAINST GOOSE GOSLIN (WHICH HE LOST, .378 TO .377)

"IN MY DAY, we were farmers. All we wanted to do was play."

—PIE TRAYNOR

"HIS LOVE WAS BASEBALL—the fans his friends, the world his playground. To play on the same club with Ruth was not only a pleasure, it was a privilege—an experience which comes once in a lifetime."

—YANKEE PITCHER WAITE HOYT, BASEBALL DIGEST, AUGUST 1961

CHAMPION OF THE LITTLE GUY

HE BROUGHT EXPLODING SCOREBOARDS, a 42-year-old rookie, and a 3′7″ pinch-hitter to the major leagues, and while he didn't mix too well with his fellow owners, he certainly gave the fans a good time. Through a wild life spent putting forth stunts, gimmicks, and some very good teams, Bill Veeck offered others the chance to enjoy the game as much as he did while living up to his Hall of Fame epitaph: "Champion of the Little Guy."

Veeck's impact on baseball began early. As a teenager working for the Chicago Cubs club owned by his father, he planted the seeds from which burst forth the ivy that still covers the outfield walls of Wrigley Field. He quit college at age 19 to become full-time treasurer of the Cubs, then was off to minor-league Milwaukee—where with the help of home-plate weddings, fireworks, and pig giveaways, he turned a moribund franchise into a club so popular it prompted Boston Braves owner Lou Perini to move his big-league team to Wisconsin a decade later. Veeck had a wooden leg courtesy of World War II, but most folks still found it impossible to keep up with "The Maverick" and his shenanigans.

It was more of the same in the majors, where Veeck actually had his office doors physically removed to encourage visitors. A shrewd judge of talent, he built a World Series champion in Cleveland by 1948. And with promotions such as "Good Ol' Joe Early" night—when he showered an average fan with gifts—demolished Yankee attendance records by drawing over 2.6 million fans. One of his wildest moves in '48 was bringing aboard ancient "rookie" pitcher and Negro League legend Satchel Paige, who went 6-1. A year earlier, when Veeck broke the American League color line by bringing Larry Doby to Cleveland, he received 20,000 letters from incensed fans and answered each by hand. After the Indians were officially eliminated from the 1949 pennant race, the Maverick led a funeral cortege onto the field and buried the club's '48 championship banner.

A few years later Veeck sold the Tribe and purchased the dismal St. Louis Browns, more than doubling attendance for a seventh-place club thanks to stunts like the 1951 appearance of No. ⅛ Eddie Gaedel—whose 3'7" frame prompted a walk on four pitches. From there it was on to the White Sox, where Veeck copped another pennant in 1959 and set club attendance marks due in part to a scoreboard that shot off fireworks following home runs. The old guard of ownership never appreciated his free spirit, but he always had the love of his players, and most importantly the fans—whom as a 70-year-old he often sat alongside in the Wrigley Field bleachers, shirtless and with his wooden leg serving as a beer coaster and ashtray.

"JOSH, I WISH YOU and Satchel [Paige] played with me on the Cardinals. Hell, we'd win the pennant by July 4 and go fishin' until World Series time."

—DIZZY DEAN TO NEGRO LEAGUER JOSH GIBSON IN 1934

"I DIDN'T HAVE NOTHIN'. . . . I had no license to beat anybody. But they coulda cut off my arm in that clubhouse if I'd won that one."

—DIZZY DEAN ON HIS 6-3 LOSS TO THE YANKEES IN GAME 2 OF THE 1938 WORLD SERIES

"WHEN I WAS A KID, I practiced eight hours a day for nothing, so why shouldn't I do the same thing when I got to be a pro?"

—HANK GREENBERG

"BETTER PUT BABE DAHLGREN on first. I'm not doing the club any good out there."

—LOU GEHRIG, TELLING YANKEE MANAGER JOE MCCARTHY TO REPLACE HIM IN THE LINEUP, ENDING HIS STRING OF 2,130 GAMES

"WE SHALL MISS HIM in the infield
And we shall miss him at the bat,
But he's true to his religion
And I honor him for that."

—POET EDGAR GUEST, TRUMPETING HANK GREENBERG'S DECISION NOT TO PLAY ON YOM KIPPUR, 1934

"FANS, FOR THE PAST two weeks you have been reading about the bad break I got. Yet today I consider myself the luckiest man on the face of the Earth."

—OPENING OF LOU GEHRIG'S FAREWELL ADDRESS AT YANKEE STADIUM, JULY 4, 1939

"I WAS HIT with 12 of the 18 pellets—nine in each barrel—and six of them went right through my legs. I've still got three of them in my abdomen. But I'll tell you, I was back pitching that next season."

—RIP SEWELL ON A 1940 POSTSEASON HUNTING ACCIDENT; HE WON 14 GAMES THE FOLLOWING SEASON

THE PRIDE OF PITTSBURGH

FOR MUCH OF HIS CAREER Roberto Clemente toiled in the shadow of stars in bigger cities, but the proud Puerto Rican outfielder would eventually be in a class by himself as a noble and tragic hero in his native and adopted lands. A steady hitter and superb fielder from his 1955 rookie season with the Pirates, Clemente was a vital cog in Pittsburgh's 1960 championship club while beginning a string of 12 consecutive Gold Glove Awards. He added his first of four batting crowns the next year, and by 1966 was National League MVP. Still, it wasn't until the 1971 World Series—when a nationwide television audience saw the 37-year-old hit .414, make several great fielding plays, and homer twice—that Clemente's talents were fully appreciated. Then, after notching his 3,000th hit in '72, Clemente was killed on New Year's Eve when the plane he was flying in to help bring relief supplies to Nicaraguan earthquake victims crashed just after takeoff. The five-year mandatory waiting period for the Hall of Fame was lifted, and Roberto Clemente took his proper spot among baseball's immortals the next summer.

"IF A BLACK BOY can make it on Okinawa and Guadalcanal,
hell, he can make it in baseball."

—BASEBALL COMMISSIONER HAPPY CHANDLER ON THE BREAKING OF
THE MAJOR-LEAGUE COLOR LINE

"I KNEW I WAS GOOD enough to play
in the big leagues. I just knew it."

—NEGRO LEAGUER JUDY JOHNSON, OUR GAME: AN AMERICAN
BASEBALL HISTORY

"MR. RICKEY, do you want a ballplayer
who's afraid to fight back?"
"I want a ballplayer with guts enough *not* to fight back!"

—EXCHANGE BETWEEN JACKIE ROBINSON AND BRANCH RICKEY ON
AUGUST 28, 1945, THE DAY ROBINSON SIGNED A BROOKLYN
CONTRACT

"BROUGHT JACKIE ROBINSON to Brooklyn in 1947."

—FINAL LINE ON BRANCH RICKEY'S HALL OF FAME PLAQUE

"THE ONLY REAL GAME in the world, I think, is baseball. . . .
You've gotta let it grow up with you, and if you're successful
and you try hard enough, you're bound to come out on top,
just like these boys have come to the top now."

—BABE RUTH, SPEAKING ON BABE RUTH DAY AT
YANKEE STADIUM, 1947

"I DON'T CARE if half the league strikes.
This is the United States of America and one citizen
has as much right to play as another."

—COMMISSIONER FORD FRICK TO CARDINALS PLAYERS, WHO HAD
BEEN PLANNING TO STRIKE WHEN THE DODGERS AND JACKIE
ROBINSON CAME TO ST. LOUIS IN 1947, THE SUMMER GAME

"TO DO WHAT he did has got to be the most tremendous
thing I've ever seen in sports."

—PEE WEE REESE ON THE ROOKIE SEASON OF DODGER TEAMMATE
JACKIE ROBINSON, THE BOYS OF SUMMER

"ABOVE ANYTHING ELSE, I hate to lose."

—JACKIE ROBINSON, GIANTS OF BASEBALL

"I WAS STARTING my major-league career with one thing in my favor, anyway. I wasn't afraid of anybody I'd see in that batting box. I'd been around too long for that."

—SATCHEL PAIGE ON HIS FEELINGS UPON JOINING THE CLEVELAND INDIANS IN 1948, MAYBE I'LL PITCH FOREVER

"WHEN BASEBALL'S NO LONGER fun, it's no longer a game. So, gentlemen, I've played my last game of ball."

—JOE DIMAGGIO, ANNOUNCING HIS RETIREMENT, DECEMBER 1951

"IF I HAVE TO WIN one game, I want something to say about it myself, so I've got to be in there."

—RALPH KINER ON WHY HE PICKED HIMSELF AS A MEMBER OF HIS "ULTIMATE LINEUP," THE GREATEST TEAM OF ALL TIME

"WHEN YOU'RE WALKING to the bank with that World Series check every November, you don't want to leave. There were no Yankees saying play me or trade me."

—HANK BAUER, A MEMBER OF NINE YANKEE WORLD SERIES WINNERS, THE ULTIMATE BASEBALL BOOK

THE ONE-ARMED OUTFIELDER

OF ALL THE MAJOR-LEAGUERS too young, too old, or otherwise unfit for military service during World War II, none had as big an impact on those who saw him perform as Browns outfielder Pete Gray. Born in Nanticoke, Pennsylvania, in 1915, Gray had lost his right arm in a farm accident at age six but taught himself to play baseball with one limb well enough to star in local semipro leagues. Possessing a great eye at the plate and daring on the basepaths, he also excelled in the outfield by using his speed and a self-taught method of catching the ball, tossing it in the air as he threw aside his glove, then catching and throwing the ball with his bare hand—all in one fluid motion.

Gray began his pro career in 1942, and two years later he was MVP of the Southern Association with a .333 average, five homers, a league record-tying 68 stolen bases, and a 1.000 outfield fielding average at Memphis. The performance made the shy bachelor a celebrity much in demand at veteran's hospitals, and earned him a spot on the 1945 defending American League champion St. Louis Browns.

Gray singled on Opening Day vs. Detroit's Hal Newhouser, but it soon became apparent the majors were too tough a challenge. Gray had trouble with changeups, outfielders played him shallow to exploit his lack of power, and he could not stop runners from taking extra bases on his arm. After hitting .218 in 77 games (yet striking out just 11 times in 234 at bats), he was back in the minors for good—but not before impressing a nation of fans with his efforts.

"THE RUTH IS MIGHTY and shall prevail. He did yesterday."

—*HEYWOOD BROUN'S LEAD TO HIS* NEW YORK WORLD *ARTICLE OF OCTOBER 12, 1923*

"FOR LOU, the game was almost holy, a religion."

—*SPORTS WRITER STANLEY FRANK ON LOU GEHRIG*

"THE COMBINATION OF SPEED and power and switch-hitting skill that he brought to baseball was rare enough, but even more rare was the stoical courage that enabled him to survive a succession of injuries that would have taxed the patience of a hero in a Greek tragedy."

—*LEE ALLEN ON MICKEY MANTLE,* THE SPORTING NEWS, *DECEMBER 8, 1968*

"THIS IS A BIGGER DAY than I've ever had before. And to think that this plaque will hang here until the end of time."

—*ELMER FLICK, IN HIS HALL OF FAME INDUCTION SPEECH, 1963*

"GOD GAVE ME an unusual arm. I've done well with it, and maybe I can keep doing well with it. I certainly don't see anything to be angry about."

—*SANDY KOUFAX'S RESPONSE WHEN ASKED IF HE WAS BITTER ABOUT HAVING ARTHRITIS AT AGE 28, THE BASEBALL LIFE OF SANDY KOUFAX*

"I'VE GOT A LOT of years to live after baseball. And I would like to live them with the complete use of my body."

—*ARTHRITIS-RIDDEN SANDY KOUFAX, ANNOUNCING HIS RETIREMENT*

"JUST TO KNOW he's in the lineup, ready to swing with somebody on base, gives a ballclub like ours a lift it needs. He is the kind of player who is so good himself, it makes everybody want to follow his example."

—*ELSTON HOWARD ON LONG-TIME YANKEE TEAMMATE MICKEY MANTLE, THE BASEBALL LIFE OF MICKEY MANTLE*

"I NEVER KNEW how someone dying could say he was the luckiest man in the world. But now I understand."

—MICKEY MANTLE, *COMPARING HIS RETIREMENT TO THAT OF LOU GEHRIG, JUNE 1969*

"I'VE TRIED TO MAKE UP for it by living as clean a life as I could. I'm proud of the way I've lived, and I think my family is, too."

—81-YEAR-OLD ED CICOTTE, *COMMENTING ON THE BLACK SOX SCANDAL 46 YEARS AFTER THE FACT*

"MY GREATEST THRILL in baseball was just putting on the uniform of a big-league ballplayer, especially for every season's opening game. I believe the joy of getting paid as a man to play a boy's game kept me going longer than many other players."

—STAN MUSIAL

"BASEBALL KIND OF GREW UP in my family, and I grew up with it. . . . . I guess it was in my blood."

—HANK AARON, HAMMERIN' HANK OF THE BRAVES

No Excuses

"I WANTED TO BE like Nolan Ryan. I didn't want to be like Pete Gray." Such were the boyhood dreams of Jim Abbott, a Flint, Michigan, native who sought a baseball career despite having a right arm that ended just above the wrist. Abbott had no intention of making the majors as an oddity, the reason many believe one-armed Gray caught on in the war-depleted summer of 1945. Abbott yearned to succeed on his talent alone, and in the end he would do so—but not without becoming a reluctant hero.

Born in 1967 just as his own hero, Ryan, was breaking in with the Mets, Abbott taught himself to transfer his glove from his left arm to his right by throwing against a brick wall. He said later that his missing hand "wasn't really an issue when I was a kid." By becoming an expert fielder, he kept hitters from using the logical tactic of bunting against him to their advantage. His college career included a 26-8 record at the University of Michigan, a win in the gold-medal game of the 1988 Olympics, and the Sullivan Award the same year as the nation's best amateur athlete.

California's No. 1 pick in the 1988 draft, Abbott became

one of a handful of players in history to completely bypass the minor leagues, then overcame a media circus to go 12-12 as a rookie with the 1989 Angels. More great moments would follow—including a 1993 no-hitter for the Yankees—and it wasn't long before he had gotten his wish; he was simply James Abbott—pitcher.

"I HOPE SO, just as I hope someone will come along and break all my records. I wouldn't want my records to just stay in the books all the time. I'd like to see someone break them. It means there's improvement."

—*HANK AARON, WHEN ASKED IN 1971 IF HE FELT HE COULD BREAK BABE RUTH'S CAREER HOME RUN RECORD, HAMMERIN' HANK OF THE BRAVES*

"IT'S A GREAT DAY for baseball. Let's play two."

—*ERNIE BANKS*

"I FEEL RIGHT most of the time, but I can't sign for hours like I did. But geez, I guess I'm lucky to be able to sign at all."

—*TED WILLIAMS, AFTER THREE STROKES, ON SIGNING AUTOGRAPHS, SPORTS ILLUSTRATED, NOVEMBER 25, 1996*

"GEORGE THOMAS SEAVER against Henry Louis Aaron—that was a game within a game for me even if he didn't know it. It was the stuff my dreams were made of ever since I began throwing the ball against the chimney, trying to get the ball in on an imaginary Henry Aaron's fists."

—*ROOKIE PITCHER TOM SEAVER ON FACING HIS IDOL FOR THE FIRST TIME IN 1967, BASEBALL IS MY LIFE*

"BASEBALL GIVES EVERY American boy the chance to excel. I hope that some day Satchel Paige and Josh Gibson will be voted into the Hall of Fame as symbols of the great Negro players who are not here only because they weren't given the chance."

—*TED WILLIAMS, IN HIS 1966 HALL OF FAME INDUCTION SPEECH*

"I DON'T WANT to take anything away from Dr. [Martin Luther] King. But through baseball, Jackie did more to segregation, hotels, and sports arenas than any other man."

—*DON NEWCOMBE, BASEBALL QUOTATIONS*

"DEAR MR. KUHN:
After twelve years in the major leagues, I do not feel
that I am a piece of property to be bought and sold
irrespective of my wishes. I believe that any system which
produces that result violates my basic rights as a
citizen and is inconsistent with the laws of the
United States and of the several States."

—CURT FLOOD'S LETTER TO BASEBALL COMMISSIONER BOWIE KUHN
ON DECEMBER 24, 1969, REQUESTING HE BE GRANTED THE RIGHT
TO CHOOSE WHICH TEAM HE WOULD PLAY FOR, THE WAY IT IS

"I WAS NOT A CONSIGNMENT of goods. I was a man, the
rightful proprietor of my own person and my own talents."

—CURT FLOOD ON REFUSING HIS TRADE FROM ST. LOUIS TO
PHILADELPHIA, THE WAY IT IS

"THE ST. GEORGE of Baseball, for he has slain the
dragon of oppression."

—THE SPORTING NEWS ON JOHN MONTGOMERY WARD, WHO
ORGANIZED THE BROTHERHOOD OF NATIONAL LEAGUE PLAYERS TO
NEGOTIATE WITH LEAGUE OWNERS IN 1889

THE IRON HORSE

WHEN BABE RUTH ADDED to his legend with his "Called Shot" home run in Game 3 of the 1932 World Series, it almost seemed fitting that Lou Gehrig's two homers in the same contest were all but lost amidst the hoopla. Playing second fiddle to the larger-than-life character who preceded him in the Yankee batting order, Gehrig was one of the few who could approach the Babe's productivity—but he often did so in Ruth's shadow.

Only as age slowed Ruth was the shy Gehrig acknowledged as the Yankees' main man. By the time Joe DiMaggio joined the club in 1936 to grab away that title, Gehrig's sturdiness had taken on a legend of its own. Since pinch-hitting on June 1, 1925, and subbing at first base for long-time Yankee Wally Pipp the following afternoon, Gehrig had not missed a single game in nearly 11 years. Pipp's reason for sitting out became known as "baseball's longest headache." By the end of the 1938 season, Gehrig had played through lumbago, broken bones, and back spasms in a record 2,122 straight contests—helping the Yanks to seven pennants and six World Series titles along the way.

Only 35 years old in the spring of 1939, the "Iron Horse" was coming off a .295, 29-homer, 114-RBI season that was a notch below his usual standards but still placed him among baseball's best. He struggled terribly at the plate during spring training and felt lethargic. His struggles continued when the season started, and after eight games in which he produced just four singles, one RBI, and two errors, he told manager Joe McCarthy he was benching himself. The streak was over at 2,130 games, but it was still hoped Gehrig would be back in the lineup once his condition improved.

A trip to the Mayo Clinic, however, ended such hopes. Gehrig was found to be suffering from amyotrophic lateral sclerosis, an illness affecting the central nervous system that causes a gradual breakdown of physical capabilities and eventually death. July 4, 1939, was declared Lou Gehrig Day at Yankee Stadium, and a smiling Lou told the packed crowd: "For the past two weeks you have been reading about what a tough break I got. But today I consider myself the luckiest man on the face of the Earth." Thousands, including Ruth, were driven to cheers and tears.

"HE NEVER BACKED DOWN from a fight, never quit agitating for equality. Those who tangled with him always admitted afterward that he was a man's man, a person who would not compromise his convictions."

—*BASEBALL WRITER WENDELL SMITH ON JACKIE ROBINSON*

". . . A KIND OF BASEBALL that none of us had ever seen before—throwing and running and hitting at something close to the level of absolute perfection, playing to win but also playing the game almost as if it were a form of punishment for everyone else on the field."

—WRITER ROGER ANGELL, DESCRIBING THE PERFORMANCE OF ROBERTO CLEMENTE IN THE 1971 WORLD SERIES, FIVE SEASONS

"I WANT TO BE REMEMBERED as a ballplayer who gave all he had to give."

—ROBERTO CLEMENTE

"YOU DON'T KNOW what's going on inside me tonight. . . . I look at the kids over here, and the way they're playing, the way they're fighting for themselves, and it tells me one thing: 'Willie, say good-bye to America.'"

—WILLIE MAYS, IN HIS FAREWELL SPEECH AT SHEA STADIUM, SEPTEMBER 25, 1973

"HAVING WILLIE STARGELL on your team is like having a diamond ring on your finger."

—PITTSBURGH MANAGER CHUCK TANNER, TIME, OCTOBER 29, 1979

"I SCORED AND LOOKED to my parents. It was the nicest thing I ever saw on a ball field when they applauded for me."

—MIKE EASLER ON SCORING THE GAME-TYING RUN IN HIS ONLY ALL-STAR GAME IN 1981, BASEBALL DIGEST, DECEMBER 1995

"IT WAS A TRUE DEFINITION of a team game, the way you were taught to play baseball. It was like a clinic. And after the game, it was like the Betty Ford clinic."

—RELIEVER LARRY ANDERSEN ON THE 1993 PHILLIES—KNOWN AS "THE WILD BUNCH," BASEBALL DIGEST, MAY 1996

"WHEN IT'S OVER, I want to say, 'Hey, I made a pretty good run. I gave it all I had.' But until that day, I'll never, ever be satisfied."

—MIKE PIAZZA

"LOOK AT IT. 'World Series. Saturday. 8 P.M.' Nice. That is nice."

—YANKEES MANAGER JOE TORRE, OBSERVING THE MARQUEE OUTSIDE YANKEES STADIUM; TORRE HAD WAITED OVER 37 YEARS AS A PLAYER AND MANAGER TO REACH HIS FIRST FALL CLASSIC, SPORTS ILLUSTRATED, OCTOBER 28, 1996

The Good with the Bad

"**H**E SAYS HELLO on opening day and good-bye on closing day, and in between he hits .350."

———*MICKEY COCHRANE ON CHARLIE GEHRINGER*

THE STREAK

WHILE MANY BASEBALL RECORDS have fallen by the wayside over the past half-century, one remains safe. Joe DiMaggio's 56-game hitting streak of 1941 has never really been approached—Pete Rose's 44-game effort in 1978 posed the nearest challenge—and this only further intensifies the scope of the accomplishment. In 56 contests from May 15 to July 16 of 1941, DiMaggio had 91 hits in 223 at bats for an average of .408. Boston fans point out that Ted Williams batted .412 over the same period, although there were several games in which Williams did not hit safely. Under increasingly intense pressure and media scrutiny, DiMaggio kept getting his hits through every road trip and doubleheader, every pitching change and nagging injury, for 56 games. It still seems a feat for the ages.

". . . UNAPPROACHABLE in his good
generalship and managership."

—NEW YORK CLIPPER *DESCRIPTION OF PLAYER-MANAGER HARRY
WRIGHT OF THE CINCINNATI RED STOCKINGS, 1869*

"[HARRY WRIGHT] EATS BASEBALL, breathes baseball, thinks baseball, dreams baseball, and incorporates baseball in his prayers."

—CINCINNATI ENQUIRER, *1869*

"[CAP] ANSON'S MAGNETISM is not stored up in every piece of human mechanism that is found on the ball field."

—CHICAGO TRIBUNE, *SEPTEMBER 13, 1885*

"FLICK IS GOING TO MAKE the outfielders hustle to hold their positions. He is the fastest and most promising youngster the Phillies have ever had."

—*SPORTS WRITER FRANCIS RICHTER ON PHILADELPHIA ROOKIE ELMER FLICK, 1898, AS QUOTED IN THE SPORTING NEWS, MARCH 23, 1963*

"[CAP] ANSON, who was our manager, was so good, in fact, that he was arrogant about it. He'd always take two strikes just to defy the pitchers, then get his hit."

—*CLARK GRIFFITH*

"THERE PROBABLY HAVE BEEN players in the game who had as much natural ability and as good a physique as [Ty] Cobb; there may also have been some—although I doubt it—who could think as fast. But there certainly never was another athlete who combined Cobb's ability and his smartness—or even came close."

—FRED HANEY

". . . A BUNDLE OF NERVES with the best brain in baseball."

—SPORTS WRITER HUGH FULLERTON ON JOHNNY EVERS

"I RECALL when [Ty] Cobb played a series with each leg a mass of raw flesh. He had a temperature of 103 and the doctors ordered him to bed for several days, but he got three hits, stole three bases, and won the game. Afterward he collapsed on the bench."

—GRANTLAND RICE, COOPERSTOWN: WHERE THE LEGENDS LIVE FOREVER

"IF I WASN'T EXPECTED to drive the ball out of the lot every time I come up there to the plate, I'd change my

batting form tomorrow. I'd copy [Ty] Cobb's style in every single thing he does."

—*BABE RUTH, BABE RUTH'S OWN BOOK OF BASEBALL*

"I AM SURE that I speak for all when I say that he has been a wholesome influence on clean living and clean sport."

—*PRESIDENT CALVIN COOLIDGE ON WALTER JOHNSON*

". . . THE PERFECT HITTER. Joe's swing was purely magical."

—*TY COBB ON JOE JACKSON*

"I MAY BE WRONG, but those fans who are booing this kid at shortstop are going to see him in this league for many years, and they'll wind up cheering him."

—*TRIS SPEAKER ON FUTURE HALL OF FAMER LUKE APPLING, THE SPORTING NEWS, JULY 25, 1964*

"IF JUDY JOHNSON were white, he could name his price."

—*CONNIE MACK ON THE TOP THIRD BASEMAN OF THE NEGRO LEAGUES DURING THE 1920S AND '30S*

DUFFY'S CLIFF AND DR. STRANGEGLOVE

SMEAD JOLLEY WAS A .313 HITTER with 114 RBI and 193 hits as a White Sox rookie in 1930, but he was nonetheless sent to the Red Sox a little over a year later when Chicago management grew tired of his poor defense at various positions. At Fenway Park, he was given the job of patrolling left field and its 37-foot wall, then fronted by a sloping hill nicknamed "Duffy's Cliff" to honor the expert ability of former Sox star Duffy Lewis to traverse it during the 1910s.

In the week before his first game, Jolley worked painstakingly with coach Eddie Collins at running up the cliff while looking skyward at fly balls. Then, when it finally counted, Jolley misjudged a line drive, fell flat on his face running down the cliff in pursuit, and had the ball bounce off his head before it rolled back toward the infield. "Ten days you guys spend teaching me how to go up the hill," Jolly said upon reaching the bench, "and there isn't one of you with the brains to teach me how to come down again." Such calamities were frequent, and despite hitting .312 with 99 RBI that year and .312 with 106 the next, Smead was let go by Boston as soon as he fell off to .282 in 1933. In the minors, where his liabilities were more accepted, he would eventually win six batting titles.

Three decades later, Jolly seemed to be resurrected in the form of Dick Stuart—a lead-footed first baseman with the Pirates whose fielding lapses earned him the nickname "Stonefingers" and overshadowed his ability to hit 20 to 30 homers per season. Flashy and egocentric, Stuart figured his offense made up for his defense and thus made no attempts to improve. Traded to the Red Sox in 1963, he fell in love with Fenway and took his slugging to a new level with 42 homers and a league-leading 118 RBI—matching this with a league-high 29 errors that were 17 more than any other American League first baseman.

Failing to recapture his RBI crown in 1964 (although he did manage 114 with 33 homers), Stuart again easily topped all comers (for the seventh straight year) with 24 miscues. Earning a new moniker of "Dr. Strangeglove" and constantly feuding with manager Johnny Pesky over his lackadaisical attitude, Stuart was sent packing before the next season.

After retirement, Stuart fondly recalled his favorite moment in the field. While manning first on a windy day in Pittsburgh, he reached out to grab a hot-dog wrapper as it blew past him, prompting a standing ovation from the fans. Ardent followers of the game, the Pirates faithful had learned that anything Stuart got to was worth acknowledging.

"Your arm is gone; your legs likewise,
But not your eyes, Mize, not your eyes."

—Writer Dan Parker after 37-year-old Johnny Mize hit 25
homers in just 274 at bats in 1950

"Sure, I believe [Sandy Koufax] has arthritis. But it doesn't
hurt from the first to the ninth inning. I know that."

—Roberto Clemente, The Baseball Life of Sandy Koufax

"Nobody is half as good as Mickey Mantle."

—Al Kaline, responding to a young boy who had said to him,
"you're not half as good as Mickey Mantle"

"To Johnny Bench, a Hall of Famer for sure."

—Inscription on ball signed by Ted Williams for
Cincinnati's 20-year-old rookie catcher,
spring training, 1968

"He's the single greatest offensive force I've seen."

—John Curtis on Lou Brock, Baseball Digest, December 1974

"If they came to Josh Gibson today and he were 17 years old, they would have a blank spot on the contract and they'd say, 'Fill the amount in.' That's how good Josh Gibson was."

—*Junior Gilliam*

"We have always been inclined to consider Ewing in his prime as the greatest player of the game . . . a player without a weakness of any kind, physical, mental or temperamental."

—*Writer Francis Richter on 19th century Hall of Famer Buck Ewing, 1919*

"[Joe] Morgan has the conviction that he should affect the outcome of every game he plays in every time he comes to bat and every time he gets on base."

—*Writer Roger Angell, Five Seasons*

"Best one-legged player I ever saw."

—*Casey Stengel on oft-injured Mickey Mantle*

BALTIMORE'S CLASS ACT

IF EVER BASEBALL NEEDED A SAVIOR, it was during the 1995 season. A 232-day strike that began August 12, 1994, had done away with the remainder of that campaign, wiped out the World Series for the first time since 1904, and continued until March 30, 1995, to force the postponement of spring training and adoption of a shortened 144-game season. Fans sick of squabbling players and owners showed their displeasure by not showing up once action resumed; attendance fell significantly, and a dark cloud hung over the game. Luckily, there was one man capable of lifting it—Cal Ripken Jr.

A fixture at shortstop for the Orioles since 1982 and a two-time MVP, Ripken resumed play in '95 needing to appear in Baltimore's first 122 contests to break Lou Gehrig's once "unbeatable" record of 2,130 consecutive games played. Anticipation grew throughout the summer, and when Ripken finally reached the magic mark in early September he added flourish to the event. Smashing a homer before a packed home crowd in game No. 2,130 September 5, he homered again the following night as he broke the record—further padding his other mark of home runs by a shortstop that would reach 319 by year's end. Celebrating in his typically classy fashion, Ripken jogged around Camden Yards shaking and high-fiving the hands of fans after No. 2,131 became official midway through the game—and for at least one moment, 50,000 folks in Baltimore and millions more watching on television could forget the malodorous atmosphere surrounding major-league baseball.

"THE POWER of the team blinded onlookers to the skill and smoothness of its fielding. Enemy teams cracked and broke wide open before their assaults."

—FRANK GRAHAM ON THE 1927 YANKEES, THE NEW YORK YANKEES

"PLEASE DON'T INTERRUPT, because you haven't heard this one before . . . honest. At precisely 4:45 P.M. today, in Yankee Stadium, off came the 52-year slur on the ability of the Dodgers to win a World Series, for at that moment the last straining Yankee was out at first base, and the day, the game, and the 1955 Series belonged to Brooklyn."

—LEAD TO SHIRLEY POVICH'S STORY IN THE WASHINGTON POST, OCTOBER 4, 1955

"No TEAM EVER looked more intense than they did. Getting on the field with them was akin to stepping into a wading pool with Jaws."

—RED SOX PITCHER BILL LEE ON THE YANKEES AFTER THEIR RECORD 14½ GAME COMEBACK IN 1978, THE WRONG STUFF

"I DON'T WANT to embarrass any other catcher by comparing them to Johnny Bench."

—SPARKY ANDERSON, 50TH ANNIVERSARY HALL OF FAME YEARBOOK

"He SEEMS to have an *obligation* to hit."

—LOU BROCK ON PETE ROSE, LATE INNINGS

"I'M IN THE BEST SHAPE of my life, and that includes my brain."

—LENNY DYKSTRA, BASEBALL DIGEST, AUGUST 1993

"So COMMON HAS BETTING become at baseball matches, that the most respectable clubs in the country indulge in it to a highly culpable degree, and so common . . . the tricks by which games have been 'sold' for the benefit of gamblers

that the most respectable of participants have been suspected of this baseness."

—HARPER'S WEEKLY, OCTOBER 26, 1867

"BUT THERE IS NO JOY in Mudville—mighty Casey has struck out."

—FINAL LINE OF ERNEST LAWRENCE THAYER'S EPIC POEM CASEY AT THE BAT: A BALLAD OF THE REPUBLIC

"ANY PROFESSIONAL BASE BALL CLUB will 'throw' a game if there is money in it. A horse race is a pretty safe thing to speculate on, in comparison with an average ball match."

—NEW YORK CLIPPER, APRIL 24, 1875

". . . WORTHLESS, DISSIPATED GLADIATOR; not much above the professional pugilist in morality and respectability. To employ professional players to perspire in public for the benefit of gamblers . . . furnishes to dyseptic moralists a strong argument against any form of muscular Christianity."

—NEW YORK TIMES EDITORIAL CONDEMNING BASEBALL AND ITS PLAYERS AS ALL THINGS EVIL, MARCH 8, 1872

MARVELOUS MARV

THE 1962 NEW YORK METS were one of the worst teams in baseball history, but also one of the most memorable. Completing their maiden season in the National League with a record of 40-120, they finished 60½ games behind San Francisco but first in the hearts of fans who still missed the pennant-winning Giants (who had departed four years earlier for the West Coast) and packed the Polo Grounds to root for their irresistibly inept replacements. The Mets had losing streaks of 11, 13, and 17 games.

Of all the has-beens and never-would-bes who suited up for that team, none symbolized Met futility more than Marv Throneberry. Once a bonus baby with the Yankees, Throneberry (whose initials were M.E.T.) was a first baseman of decent power and friendly disposition who always seemed to do the wrong thing at the most inopportune times. His 17 errors at first topped the league, and his baserunning miscues were legendary.

On June 17 "Marvelous Marv" had his finest day; on defense he smashed into a baserunner for an interference call that led to four unearned runs, and on offense he smashed a triple only to be called out for failing to touch first base. When manager Casey Stengel came out

to protest, he was intercepted by coach Cookie Lavagetto, who whispered words that summed up New York's season: "Forget it, Case. He didn't touch second either." The Mets, of course, lost 8-7—Marvelous Marv striking out with the winning run on base to end it.

"THE FEMALE HAS NO PLACE in baseball,
except to the degradation of the game."

—*VIEW ON A RECENTLY FORMED WOMEN'S PRO TEAM,*
ST. LOUIS GLOBE-DEMOCRAT, APRIL 11, 1886

". . . THE TOUGHEST of the toughs and an abomination of the diamond . . . a rough, unruly man . . . he uses every low and contemptible method that his erratic brain can conceive to win a play by a dirty trick."

—*UMPIRE JOHN HEYDLER ON PLAYER-MANAGER*
JOHN MCGRAW, 1890s

"IT DEPENDS on the length of the game."

—*KING KELLY'S RESPONSE TO A REPORTER ASKING IF HE EVER DRANK*
WHILE PLAYING, LATE 19TH CENTURY

"I COULD FIELD the ball all right, but on the throw I couldn't hit the first baseman or anything near him."

—JOHN McGRAW ON HIS EARLY DAYS AS A 16-YEAR-OLD MINOR-LEAGUER

"I BELIEVE THE SALE of Babe Ruth will ultimately strengthen the team."

—RED SOX OWNER HARRY FRAZEE, WHO IN JANUARY 1920 SOLD THE GREATEST PLAYER IN BASEBALL HISTORY TO THE YANKEES

"I DON'T ROOM with him; I room with his suitcase."

—YANKEE BIG BODIE ON HIS MISCHIEVOUS TEAMMATE/ROOMMATE BABE RUTH, BABE: THE LEGEND COMES TO LIFE

"HE HAS a corkscrew brain."

—JIM PRICE OF THE NEW YORK PRESS DESCRIBING HAL CHASE, KNOWN TO FIX GAMES IN WHICH HE PLAYED

"HE HAD LARCENY in his heart but his feet were honest."

—SPORTS WRITER BUGS BAER ON SLOW-FOOTED PING BODIE

"SHALL I GET YOU a net, or do you want a basket?"

—RED SOX SHORTSTOP HEINIE WAGNER NEEDLING GIANTS SHORTSTOP
ART FLETCHER DURING THE SECOND GAME OF THE 1912 WORLD
SERIES; FLETCHER HAD MADE THREE ERRORS IN THE CONTEST

"YOU KNOW I CAN'T EAT tablets or nicely
framed awards. Neither can my wife.
But they don't think of things like that."

—PENNILESS GROVER CLEVELAND ALEXANDER ON THE REPLICA
TABLET HE RECEIVED FROM COOPERSTOWN FOLLOWING HIS 1939
HALL OF FAME INDUCTION, BASEBALL AS I HAVE KNOWN IT

"WITH THIS BATTING SLUMP I'm in, I was so happy
to hit a double that I did a tap dance on second base.
They tagged me between taps."

—FRENCHY BORDAGARAY OF THE DODGERS

"WE HAD A LOT of triple-threat
guys—slip, fumble, and fall."

—PITTSBURGH CATCHER JOE GARAGIOLA ON THE AWFUL PIRATE
TEAMS OF THE EARLY 1950s

WHAT'S SO FUNNY?

CASEY STENGEL SUMMED UP the life of Yogi Berra thusly: "They say he's funny. Well, he has a lovely wife and family, a beautiful home, money in the bank, and he plays golf with millionaires. What's funny about that?" Casey was right about his clutch-hitting catcher; Lawrence Peter Berra was a superstar who experienced fame and fortune and had the good sense to keep his life in perspective. Still, he was always looked at as a comical figure rather than a fortuitous one—thanks to the stocky appearance that earned him his nickname and his knack for comments that made no sense and total sense at the same time. A popular restaurant was "so crowded nobody goes there anymore," while an inexperienced manager could "observe a lot by watching." Berra grasped the art of catching when Yankee great Bill Dickey "learned me all his experiences," and nobody ever offered a more accurate assessment of competitive sports: "It ain't over till it's over." Nothing funny about that kind of thinking.

"MR. GEORGE H. RUTH:
You are hereby notified as follows:
1. That you are unconditionally released.
—Jacob Ruppert"

—*LETTER BABE RUTH SUPPOSEDLY RECEIVED FROM YANKEE OWNER RUPPERT IN FEBRUARY 1935*

"I DON'T THINK either of them can win."

—COLUMNIST WARREN BROWN WHEN ASKED WHICH TEAM HE
THOUGHT WOULD WIN THE 1945 WORLD SERIES MATCHUP
BETWEEN WAR-DILUTED DETROIT AND CHICAGO,
BASEBALL DIGEST, AUGUST 1971

"SIXTY THOUSAND FANS cheering like mad and the 'Great DiMag' stood there taking bows. Next thing I knew, Frankie Crosetti was racing toward me, frantically waving his arms. . . . Frankie wanted the ball."

—JOE DIMAGGIO ON HIS MOST EMBARRASSING MOMENT, THE TIME
HE MADE A GREAT CATCH AND DIDN'T REALIZE THERE WAS ONLY ONE
OUT AND A MAN ON FIRST BASE AT THE TIME,
BASEBALL DIGEST, AUGUST 1971

"JIM GENTILE WAS 6'4", weighed 215 pounds, and every year almost managed to make the number of runs he knocked in with his bat equal the number of runs he let in with his glove. He always looked to me like a low echelon commanding officer of a particularly inefficient Army unit."

—FROM THE GREAT AMERICAN BASEBALL CARD FLIPPING,
TRADING AND BUBBLE GUM BOOK

"Can't anybody here play this game?"

—Manager Casey Stengel on his 1962 Mets team, which went 40-120

"I'm leaving the same way I came—with nothing."

—373-game winner Grover Cleveland Alexander, who had drunk away the money earned in a 20-year big-league career

"The Mets achieved total incompetence in a single year, while the Browns worked industriously for almost a decade to gain equal proficiency."

—Bill Veeck, Veeck: As in Wreck

"DUROCHER ILLUSTRATES the way in which being a sleazbag can keep you out of the Hall of Fame."

—BILL JAMES ON SUCCESSFUL BUT OBNOXIOUS MANAGER LEO DUROCHER, THE POLITICS OF GLORY

"GEEZ, they told me he couldn't hit but they forgot to tell me he couldn't catch, either."

—METS MANAGER CASEY STENGEL ON CHRIS CANNIZZARO—ONE OF THE SEVEN CATCHERS HE USED IN THE CLUB'S MAIDEN 40-120 SEASON, BASEBALL DIGEST, APRIL 1975

"PEOPLE FOUND HUMOR in the way the Mets lost or—rarely—won. I suppose it would have been gentler for that team to play in privacy."

—TOM SEAVER ON THE '62 METS, BASEBALL IS MY LIFE

"ERRORS ARE PART of my image. One night in Pittsburgh, 30,000 fans gave me a standing ovation when I caught a hot dog wrapper on the fly."

—FIRST BASEMAN DICK STUART, KNOWN AS "DR. STRANGEGLOVE," PLAYING THE FIELD

A "Can't Miss" Who Missed

Players described as "can't miss" prospects rarely live up to
their hype and type. But seldom has bold forecasting proved
so wrong as in the case of Clint Hartung. Heralded as the
next coming of George Herman Ruth, Hartung had gone
25-0 pitching and hit .567 with 30 homers in 57 games
overall for a service team during World War II—enough to
convince the pennant-hungry Giants to sign him and writers to dub him the "Hondo Hurricane" in deference to his
native Hondo, Texas. By the end of Hartung's first spring
training in 1947, it was apparent his skills and advance
notice were not equal, and he even-
tually racked up a 29-29 pitching record and .238 batting
average in parts of six seasons. His overhyped billing,
however, set a new standard,
and that, and that alone, has
kept the name "Clint Hartung"
recognizable to baseball fans.

"Don Buddin should have 'E6' on his license plate."

—*Sports writer Cliff Keane on the error-prone Red Sox
shortstop*, The Picture History of the Boston Red Sox

"I HAVE TROUBLE remembering my wedding anniversary, but I remember those four pitches. I remember I got a big hand from the crowd when I left."

—*TIGERS PITCHER PAUL FOYTACK, RECALLING THE FOUR STRAIGHT HOME RUNS HE ALLOWED IN THE SIXTH INNING OF A GAME AT CLEVELAND*

"IF HE'S PLAYED that many games without an error, he isn't going after the hard ones. The fellow who never makes a mistake is the fellow who never does anything."

—*TIGERS MANAGER HUGH JENNINGS UPON BEING TOLD A MINOR-LEAGUE PROSPECT HAD PLAYED 87 STRAIGHT ERRORLESS GAMES*

"THE REASON BASEBALL has no black managers is that I truly believe that they may not have some of the necessities to be, let's say, a field manager."

—*DODGERS EXECUTIVE AL CAMPANIS, INTERVIEWED BY TED KOPPEL ON ABC'S NIGHTLINE ON THE 40TH ANNIVERSARY OF JACKIE ROBINSON'S MAJOR-LEAGUE DEBUT, APRIL 1987; CAMPANIS WAS FIRED SHORTLY THEREAFTER*

MATTY: ALL-AMERICAN HERO

IN THE SAME WAY iron men Lou Gehrig and Cal Ripken came to symbolize the best in class and competence during their respective eras, Christy Mathewson was known in the years immediately following 1900 as both baseball's finest pitcher and its premier gentleman—a combination helping to dispel notions that ballplayers were rubes or roughians unsuitable for mixing with polite society. "Mathewson altered turn-of-the-century conceptions about men who played the game," wrote Tom Meany of the New York *World Telegram*. "Through him, the public learned that a professional ballplayer need be neither a hayseed nor a tough-talking, tobacco-chewing, whiskey-guzzling refugee from the poolrooms of the teeming cities."

One of the first college boys to star in the majors, the 19-year-old Mathewson came to the Giants for a few games in 1900 via Bucknell University (where he was class president and a football kicker), then in his first full season of '01 won 20 games with a 2.41 ERA. The 6'1", blond-haired and blue-eyed son of prosperous farmers was as modest as he was proficient, and teammates whose backgrounds and makeup differed vastly from his own took to him immediately. Manager John McGraw came to New York in mid-1902, and his own quick liking to Mathewson helped "Matty" take his game to a higher level. From 1903 to 1905, the right-hander won 30 or more games with league-leading strikeout totals each season, capping the string with an incredible 31-9 record in '05 punctuated with a 1.28 ERA and three shutout victories in the World Series.

More outstanding seasons would follow—37-11 with 11 shutouts in 1908, a 1.14 ERA in 1909—with Mathewson using pinpoint control and an ancient form of the screwball he termed his "fadeaway" to continuously baffle National League batsmen. He replaced speed with smarts as his career wound down, and in 1916 he retired as the winningest pitcher in NL history with a 373-188 record, a 2.13 lifetime ERA, and just 844 walks allowed over 4,780⅔ innings. How cool-headed was he? In 635 lifetime games, he was never thrown out of a contest, and legend has it that umpires so respected his honesty that they would sometimes ask his opinion on close plays.

Further befitting his heroic stature, the 38-year-old Mathewson enlisted as an Army captain in World War I. While serving overseas, he was gassed in a training exercise. He suffered from tuberculosis thereafter, and despite returning to coach with the Giants in 1919 and 1920 and serving as part-time president of the Braves in 1923, he spent much of his time in upstate New York sanitariums battling his affliction. He remained the game's most luminous star even as his health began flickering out, and when his death at age 45 was announced before the second game of the 1925 World Series, players on both sides donned black armbands for a fallen hero.

Big Bats and Hard Hurlers

"RUTH MADE A GRAVE MISTAKE when he gave up pitching. Working once a week, he might have lasted a long time and become a great star."

—*TRIS SPEAKER ON BABE RUTH'S SWITCH TO THE OUTFIELD, 1919*

THE SHOT HEARD AROUND THE WORLD

MANY BASEBALL FANS CAN ADMIT to youthful fantasies of hitting a World Series-winning home run, but the feat did not occur from 1903 until 1960, when Bill Mazeroski of the Pirates sent the Yankees home. Joe Carter of the Blue Jays in 1993 was also able to play out his boyhood dreams as a grown man. But ranking just behind their blasts on the list of holy homers is a classic bomb that had nearly as much impact and arguably more drama attached to it.

The 1951 Brooklyn Dodgers looked by all accounts to be a team of destiny. Runners-up to the Yankees in the World Series of 1947 and 1949, the team later immortalized as "The Boys of Summer" had lost the pennant on the final day the previous season— then went out and added left fielder Andy Pafko to a lineup already containing future Hall of Famers Jackie Robinson, Duke Snider, Pee Wee Reese, and Roy Campanella. The Dodgers took a 13½-game lead over the Giants by August 11, but the New Yorkers began a 16-game win streak the next day that sparked an incredible 39-8 stretch run. This enabled them to tie Brooklyn (which had continued to play .600 ball) at the wire and force a best-of-three subway playoff series. After the clubs split the first two contests, the Dodgers seemed to have things in hand with ace Don Newcombe on the mound and a 4-1 lead in the last of the ninth inning of Game 3 at the Polo Grounds.

Fate had other things in store. Letting up singles to Alvin Dark and Don Mueller (the second of which some Dodger fans argued would have been a double play had first baseman Gil Hodges been correctly positioned off the bag), Newcombe managed to get dangerous Monte Irvin to pop up for the first out. Whitey Lockman then doubled to make it 4-2; after much discussion on the mound, Newcombe was removed. Tension built as Brooklyn swingman Ralph Branca warmed up in anticipation of facing Giants slugger Bobby Thomson—who had already homered off him in the first game. On deck was a nervous rookie named Willie Mays. As the count went to 1-and-0, radios throughout New York City were tuned in to hear play-by-play man Russ Hodges scream himself hoarse calling the game's final pitch:

"Branca throws . . . . There's a long drive! It's going to be, I believe! The Giants win the pennant! The Giants win the pennant! The Giants win the pennant! The Giants win the pennant!"

It was called "The Shot Heard Around the World," and over 40 years later, countless fans still remember where they were when Thomson went deep.

". . . TOUCHED MOTHER EARTH 60 feet from the fence
on the outside of the grounds. Then it galloped
up Calvert Street and assaulted a Blue Line car."

—*A DESCRIPTION OF A HOMER HIT BY SLUGGER DAN BROUTHERS OF
THE BALTIMORE ORIOLES, 1890S*

"I WOULD BE the laughingstock of the league
if I took the best left-handed pitcher in the league
and put him in the outfield."

—*RED SOX MANAGER ED BARROW IN 1918 ON MOVING BABE RUTH
FROM THE MOUND TO A FULL-TIME POSITION, THE SPORTING NEWS,
JANUARY 16, 1965*

"SIXTY. COUNT 'EM. Sixty!
Let's see some other SOB match that!"

—*BABE RUTH IN THE YANKEE LOCKER ROOM AFTER HITTING HIS
60TH HOMER OF THE SEASON, SEPTEMBER 30, 1927, CLOUT! THE
TOP HOME RUNS IN BASEBALL HISTORY*

"HECK, IF I'D A KNOWN it was going to be
a famous record, I'd a stuck it in his ear."

—*TOM ZACHARY, AFTER ALLOWING BABE RUTH'S 60TH HOMER OF
THE 1927 SEASON, RAIN DELAYS*

"One of the secrets of the Babe's greatness was that he never lost any of his enthusiasm for playing ball, and especially for hitting home runs. To him a homer was a homer, whether he hit it in a regular game, a World Series game, or an exhibition game."

—*Sports writer Frank Graham on Babe Ruth,*
The New York Yankees

"When he retired with 714, he had more than twice as many as the second man on the list. The home run was his."

—*Robert Creamer on Babe Ruth,*
Babe: The Legend Comes to Life

"A base hit meant more to [Cap] Anson than a week's pay."

—*Grantland Rice*

"A Lajoie with Cobb's speed might have batted .500."

—*Grantland Rice*

THAT CLOSE

THE SUMMER-LONG PURSUIT by Yankees Roger Maris and
Mickey Mantle of Babe Ruth's home run record in 1961 is
usually remembered simply for its end result—54 dingers
for the Mick and 61 (and an asterisk) for Roger. Forgotten
is just how close Maris came to tying Ruth within the 154
games that Commissioner Ford Frick designated "worthy"
of the true record in light of that year's expansion to a 162-
game season. Maris entered the 154th contest at Baltimore—birthplace of the Babe—with 58 homers, and in the
third inning that afternoon hit No. 59 off Milt Pappas.
Maris now had three at bats to match Ruth. In the fourth,
Maris struck out against Dick Hall, and in the seventh,
Roger hit one shot to right that curved 10 feet foul and
another knocked down by wind and caught in front of the
railing in right-center. In the ninth, facing knuckleballer
Hoyt Wilhelm, Maris grounded out. Pretty darn close.

"BEFORE RUTH LEFT THE PLATE and started his swing around
the bases, he paused to laugh at the Chicago players,
suddenly silent in their dugout. As he rounded first he flung
a remark at Grimm; as he turned second he tossed a jest at

Billy Herman; and his shoulders shook with
satisfaction as he trotted in."

—*Sports writer Richard Vidmer of the New York Herald
Tribune, describing Babe Ruth's trot following his "Called
shot" homer vs. the Cubs in the 1932 World Series, as
quoted in Baseball Digest, October 1957*

"**All** I want out of life is that when I walk down the
street people will say, 'There goes the greatest hitter who
ever lived.'"

—*Red Sox rookie Ted Williams*

"**What** was Lombardi's lifetime? Three-oh-six? Well, if he
had normal speed, he would have made batting marks that
would still be on the books."

—*Ted Williams on catcher Ernie Lombardi,
The Sporting News, July 15, 1967*

"**Cadillacs** are down at the end of the bat."

—*Slugger Ralph Kiner on the value of home run hitting,
National Baseball Hall of Fame Museum Yearbook*

"NOBODY TAUGHT ME about hitting. I learned."

—*TED WILLIAMS, VOICES FROM COOPERSTOWN*

"I TOLD CRONIN I didn't want that.
If I couldn't hit .400 all the way, I didn't deserve it."

—*TED WILLIAMS ON HIS RESPONSE TO RED SOX MANAGER JOE CRONIN'S OFFER TO SIT OUT THE FINAL TWO GAMES OF THE 1941 SEASON SO HIS .39955 BATTING AVERAGE COULD BE ROUNDED UP TO .400; WILLIAMS WENT 6-FOR-8 IN A DOUBLEHEADER TO FINISH AT .406, MY TURN AT BAT*

"BRANCA THROWS. . . . There's a long drive! It's going to be . . . I do believe! The Giants win the pennant! The Giants win the pennant! The Giants win the pennant!"

—*RADIO BROADCASTER RUSS HODGES, DESCRIBING BOBBY THOMSON'S HOMER TO WIN THE 1951 NL TITLE FOR THE GIANTS, OCTOBER 3, 1951*

"I'M GOING HOME and try to get a good night's sleep. The World Series starts tomorrow."

—*BOBBY THOMSON OF THE GIANTS ON HIS PLANS IMMEDIATELY FOLLOWING HIS "SHOT HEARD AROUND THE WORLD"*

"AFTER THE GAME, it took me 20 minutes to walk to where he had hit the ball in a split second."

—*YANKEE ACE LEFTY GOMEZ ON A HOMER HE ALLOWED TO JIMMIE FOXX*

"THE YANKS, with [Babe] Ruth and [Lou] Gehrig, carry a wallop which makes [Jack] Dempsey's left hook and [Gene] Tunney's right to the body look like a gentle pat."

—*WALTER TRUMBULL OF THE NEW YORK POST, COMPARING NEW YORK'S INCOMPARABLE SLUGGERS TO THE TWO GREAT PRIZEFIGHTERS OF THE DAY*

"IT'S MORE TIMING than anything else. You don't have to be real big. Time it right, and the ball will go far enough."

—*HENRY AARON ON HITTING HOMERS, YOUNG BASEBALL CHAMPIONS*

"HOW DO I PITCH him? I wish I could throw the ball under the plate."

—*DON NEWCOMBE ON HANK AARON, YOUNG BASEBALL CHAMPIONS*

MANTLE'S MAMMOTH BLAST

BACK WHEN BABE RUTH, Hank Greenberg, and Jimmie Foxx were blasting baseballs out of parks, there was no real attempt to accurately measure the length of home runs. Not until April 17, 1953, were the words "tape-measure shot" ever uttered in reference to a homer. That afternoon, in Washington's Griffith Stadium, 20-year-old Yankee center fielder Mickey Mantle added the expression to baseball's vernacular with one swing of his bat.

Facing Senators lefty Chuck Stobbs in the top of the fifth inning, the switch-hitting Mantle took position on the right side of the plate and dug in. Not offering at the first pitch, he met the second dead-on with a tremendous cut that launched the ball on a fast climb to left-center field. It cleared the bleachers, nicked off the upper-right side of a beer sign atop an old football scoreboard (approximately 460 feet from home plate), then disappeared from view. The tiny crowd of 4,206 in the stadium was stunned, but one man acted fast. Running out of the press box and into the streets behind left field, Yankee PR director Arthur "Red" Patterson found a 10-year-old kid with the ball and asked where he found it. Taken to a yard on an adjacent street, Patterson paced off 105 feet from there to the base of the wall behind the bleachers. The final estimated distance of 565 feet was reported in the papers the next day—and the tape-measure homer was born.

"LIKE A FEATHER caught in a vortex, Williams ran around the square of bases at the center of our beseeching screaming. He ran as he always ran out home runs—hurriedly, unsmiling, head down, as if our praise were a storm of rain to get out of. He didn't tip his cap."

—WRITER JOHN UPDIKE ON TED WILLIAMS'S FINAL MAJOR-LEAGUE AT BAT, THE NEW YORKER

"ALL I COULD THINK about was, 'We beat the Yankees! We beat the Yankees!' I was in a kind of daze."

—PIRATE BILL MAZEROSKI ON HIS THOUGHTS AS HE ROUNDED THE BASES FOLLOWING HIS WORLD SERIES-WINNING HOME RUN IN 1960, CLOUT! THE TOP HOME RUNS IN BASEBALL HISTORY

"I THINK THE BALL disintegrated on the way to the plate and the catcher put it back together again. I swear, when it went past the plate it was just the spit that went by."

—SAM CRAWFORD ON ED WALSH'S SPITTER

"I've hit a lot of balls harder, but I can't say that any of them had more behind it than that one. To come off the bench and do that, after the ovation those people had given me . . . well, I can't express myself well enough to tell you how it felt."

—MICKEY MANTLE, RECALLING HIS PINCH-HIT HOMER AGAINST THE ORIOLES ON AUGUST 4, 1963, HIS FIRST AT BAT SINCE BREAKING HIS FOOT TWO MONTHS EARLIER, BASEBALL DIGEST, AUGUST 1974

"I just didn't feel like a 60-home run hitter. I was just hot and in the groove and the home runs were coming."

—REGGIE JACKSON ON HIS 1969 SEASON, WHEN HE HAD 39 HOMERS BY THE END OF JULY, BASEBALL DIGEST, JANUARY 1974

"It could be. . . . It might be. . . . It is! A home run!"

—BROADCASTER HARRY CARAY'S SIGNATURE CALL

"That's the first thing I can remember about him—the sound when he'd get a hold of one. It was just different, that's all."

—LARRY GARDNER ON BABE RUTH

"THE ONLY MISTAKE I made in my whole baseball career was hitting .361 that one year, because ever since then people have expected me to keep doing it."

—*TIGERS SLUGGER NORM CASH, WHO AFTER BATTING .361 IN 1961 NEVER HIT ABOVE .283 IN 13 MORE SEASONS, BEHIND THE MASK*

"SO I SWING, and would you believe it's a bases-loaded home run? I really sped around those bases to get back to the dugout and those candy bars in a hurry."

—*RON SANTO ON HITTING WHILE HAVING A DIABETIC REACTION*

"HE HIT HIS 700TH home run in 1934. When he hit it, only two others had more than 300 . . . the home run was his."

—*ROBERT CREAMER ON BABE RUTH, BABE: THE LEGEND COMES TO LIFE*

"HERE'S THE PITCH by Downing. . . . Swinging. . . . There's a drive into left-center field! That ball is gonna beee . . . outta here! It's gone! It's 715! There's a new home run champion of all time, and it's Henry Aaron!"

—*BROADCASTER MILO HAMILTON, APRIL 8, 1974*

HISTORY'S HARDEST THROWER

THE RADAR GUN IS A RELATIVELY modern device. Before its addition to the briefcases of major-league scouts and coaches, the most common way to judge speed was simply by watching pitchers throw. Efforts were made to find more accurate measurements—Bob Feller raced his fastball against a motorcycle—but most often the judgment of batters and scouts carried the most weight. And in the eyes of those who saw Feller, Nolan Ryan, and every other hard thrower of the past half-century, the fastest of them all was Steve Dalkowski.

His name doesn't ring a bell for most fans, because he never spent a day in the majors. Through nine seasons in the Orioles organization, he struggled with horrible wildness. He averaged an incredible 13 strikeouts and 13 walks per nine innings. Year after year, in nine different minor leagues, the left-hander toiled while Baltimore management waited for him to turn it around. The numbers were amazing—262 strikeouts and 262 walks in 170 innings during 1960, 283 pitches thrown in one game. Legends grew about the time he tore the ear off a batter with one pitch and shattered an umpire's mask with another. In 1964, his control suddenly improved and he was given a serious look by the Orioles in spring training. He blew a pitch by recently retired Ted Williams, who said simply, "Fastest ever." Then, weeks away from his making the big club, Dalkowski's arm went dead without warning on a routine throw to first. It never came around, and 20 years later he was a cotton-picker by day and a hanger-on at minor-league ballparks by night—just another face in the crowd.

"THAT'S A LOT of bombs. The stars and planets
have to be lined up just right for that "

—MO VAUGHN OF THE RED SOX ON THE POSSIBILITY OF SOMEONE
TOPPING ROGER MARIS'S RECORD OF 61 HOMERS IN A SEASON

"YOU DO HAVE the ability to take the ball and hit it the
other way. But when pitchers do come inside on that
inner third, and you hit it, that's where major-league
history is made."

—TED WILLIAMS, GIVING ADVICE TO TONY GWYNN

"A SURGE OF JOY flooded over me that I shall never forget. I felt like shouting out that I had made a ball curve; I wanted to tell everybody; it was too good to keep to myself."

—CANDY CUMMINGS, WHO CLAIMED TO HAVE INVENTED THE FIRST CURVEBALL AROUND 1864, "HOW I CURVED THE FIRST BALL"

"SCOLD HIM, find fault with him and he could not pitch at all. Praise him and he was unbeatable."

—FORMER CHICAGO MANAGER CAP ANSON ON HALL OF FAME PITCHER "SENSITIVE JOHN" CLARKSON, THE SPORTING NEWS, APRIL 6, 1963

"ALLEN SUTTON SOTHORON pitched his initials off today."

—LEAD IN ST. LOUIS NEWSPAPER, 1920S, QUOTED IN THE PITCHER

"I PITCHED 874 major-league games in 22 years, and I never had a sore arm until the day I quit. My arm went bad in 1912 when I was in spring training, and I guess it was about time."

—CY YOUNG

"YOU CAN HAVE IT. It wouldn't do me any good."

—RAY CHAPMAN TO UMPIRE BILLY EVANS AFTER TAKING TWO
STRIKES FROM WALTER JOHNSON IN 1915; HE HAD ALREADY
BEEN ON HIS WAY TO THE DUGOUT WHEN EVANS INFORMED
HIM HE STILL HAD ONE STRIKE

"YOU CAN'T HIT what you can't see."

—JOHN DALEY AFTER PINCH-HITTING AGAINST
WALTER JOHNSON IN 1912

"CAN I THROW HARDER than Joe Wood?
Listen, my friend, there's no man alive who
can throw harder than Smokey Joe Wood."

—WALTER JOHNSON

". . . AS I TOOK the position, I felt a strange relationship
between myself and that pitcher's mound. . . . It seemed to
be the most natural thing in the world to start pitching—
and to start striking out batters."

—BABE RUTH ON HIS FIRST TIME PITCHING AT ST. MARY'S
INDUSTRIAL SCHOOL FOR BOYS, THE BABE RUTH STORY

Sherry's Advice

As he arrived for training camp with the Dodgers in the spring of 1961, Sandy Koufax's career big-league pitching record stood at 36-40. Despite a devastating fastball, the 25-year-old left-hander had always lacked control—and he knew after six sub-par seasons that he didn't have many chances left. Also in camp was reserve catcher Norm Sherry, a nondescript but perceptive ballplayer who after careful study suggested Koufax was putting too much force behind each pitch. Sherry's advice was to ease up on the fast ones and throw more changeups and 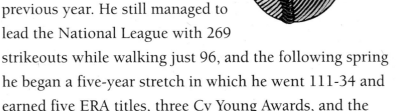 curves; Koufax took it and went 18-13 during the 1961 season—a nice boost from his 8-13 slate the previous year. He still managed to lead the National League with 269 strikeouts while walking just 96, and the following spring he began a five-year stretch in which he went 111-34 and earned five ERA titles, three Cy Young Awards, and the 1963 MVP trophy.

"... THE SADDEST WORDS of all to a pitcher are three: 'Take him out.'"

—*Christy Mathewson*, Pitching in a Pinch

"Son, I won more games than you'll ever see."

—*Cy Young, responding to a youthful reporter*

"As a pitcher, he was as mean and persistent as a bulldog with a good grip on the seat of an adversary's trousers. He was a horse for work and his idea of an intentional pass was four brushbacks."

—*Sports writer Lee Allen on Burleigh Grimes,*
The Sporting News, October 10, 1964

"Me 'n Paul's gonna win 45 games."

—*Dizzy Dean's prediction for himself and his brother*
Paul in 1934; they won 49, Cooperstown:
Where the Legends Live Forever

"If I'd known Paul was gonna do it, I'd done it, too."

—*Dizzy Dean's comment after watching his brother Paul*
pitch a no-hitter in the nightcap of a doubleheader
sweep at Brooklyn in 1934; Diz had pitched a
three-hitter in the first contest

"**O**L' SATCH THREW a lot of things, but my natural stuff was always good enough. I didn't need any spit to help out."

—*SATCHEL PAIGE, MAYBE I'LL PITCH FOREVER*

"**M**AYBE A PITCHER'S first strikeout is like your first kiss— they say you never forget it."

—*BOB FELLER, NOW PITCHING, BOB FELLER*

"**H**EY, MAC, didn't that one sound a bit low?"

—*LEFTY GOMEZ TO THE UMPIRE AFTER TAKING A CALLED STRIKE THREE FROM BOB FELLER, YOUNG BASEBALL CHAMPIONS*

"**S**PAHN AND SAIN and pray for rain."

—*JINGLE COINED DURING THE 1948 SEASON, WHEN BRAVES PITCHERS WARREN SPAHN AND JOHNNY SAIN WON NINE GAMES IN A 21-DAY STRETCH IN SEPTEMBER*

"**J**UST BEFORE I THREW the last pitch to Mitchell, I said to myself, 'Well, here goes nothing.'"

—*DON LARSEN, RECALLING HIS PERFECT GAME IN THE 1956 WORLD SERIES, BASEBALL DIGEST, JUNE 1961*

"Is that the best game you ever pitched?"

—*Question posed by an anonymous reporter to Don Larsen following his perfect World Series game in 1956*

"Against that guy, we should all get four strikes."

—*Anonymous batter on facing Sandy Koufax*

"To know for sure, I'd have to throw with a normal hand, and I've never tried it."

—*Mordecai "Three Finger" Brown, when asked if his curveball was aided by the mangled fingers on his pitching hand*

"There's a guy who could really throw that onion."

—*Babe Ruth on Walter Johnson*

"You ain't gonna get nothin' but fastballs, so don't look for anything else, and be ready."

—*Cards ace Dizzy Dean, yelling to Braves batters as they approached the plate; Dean won 13-0*

THE DAFFY DIZZY DEAN

"IF YOU SAY YOU'RE GOING to do it, and you go out and do it, it ain't bragging." Jay Hanna Dean lived by this credo throughout his colorful National League pitching career, and usually proved it right. He may have lived up to his nickname of "Dizzy" with the humorous way he mangled the English language and cavorted on and off the field, but this was one country boy who could back up his actions with heroics matched by few performers before or since.

Dubbed "Dizzy" by an Army sergeant for his quirky way of viewing the world, the right-hander was already making headlines for showing up late, trash-talking veterans, and striking out batters in bunches by the time he reached his first spring training with the Cardinals in 1931. Within two years, at the ripe age of 22, he was a 20-game winner and owned the major-league record with 17 whiffs in one game.

Dean really hit his prime in 1934, the year brother Paul joined him in the Cardinals rotation. "Me 'n Paul will win 45 games," Diz quipped, and while some scoffed, the duo was more than up to the task. Mild-mannered Paul went 19-11, his "veteran" brother 30-7 despite twice holding sit-down strikes—once to get Paul a raise on his $3,000 salary. In September, the Deans started both ends of a double-header against Brooklyn; when Paul threw a no-hitter in the nightcap, Diz told writers, "Gee, if I'd known Paul was gonna do it, I'd done it, too." He had held the Dodgers hitless until the eighth inning before settling for a three-hitter.

The Deans each won two games in the World Series for the victorious Cards that fall, but Dizzy's days at the top were numbered. A line drive off the bat of Cleveland's Earl Averill in the '37 All-Star Game broke Dean's big toe, and by coming back too soon and altering his motion he developed a sore arm. He hung on gamely for a few more years, then turned to a highly successful broadcasting career where he described how runners "slud into third," mediocre pitchers had "nothin' on the ball 'cept a cover," and weak batters "couldn't get a hit with a hoe." After repeatedly poking fun at the hapless 1947 Browns on radio, he was dared by club president Bill DeWitt to do better. Coming out of a six-year retirement for one day to throw four shutout innings, he proved himself right a final time.

"NOTHING MAKES A PITCHER feel more secure than the sight of his teammates circling the bases during a ballgame."

—*RELIEVER JIM BROSNAN, PENNANT RACE*

"WHEN WADDELL HAD CONTROL—and some sleep— he was unbeatable."

—*BRANCH RICKEY ON CAROUSING PITCHER RUBE WADDELL*

"IF YOU HAD A PILL that would guarantee a pitcher 20 wins but might take five years off his life, he'd take it."

—FORMER 20-GAME WINNER JIM BOUTON, BALL FOUR

"RYAN IS THE ONLY GUY who puts fear in me. Not because he can get you out, but because he can kill you."

—REGGIE JACKSON ON NOLAN RYAN DURING THE 1974 SEASON, DURING A STRETCH IN WHICH RYAN STRUCK OUT 1,079 AND WALKED 521 IN A THREE-YEAR SPAN

"WHEN STEVE AND I die, we're going to be buried 60 feet, six inches apart."

—TIM MCCARVER, STEVE CARLTON'S "PERSONAL" CATCHER MUCH OF HIS CAREER, THE PITCHER

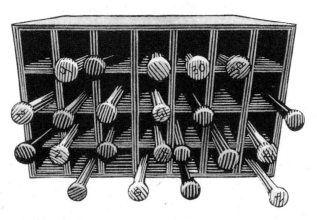

"WHEN THEY OPERATED, I told them to put in a Koufax fastball. They did—but it was Mrs. Koufax's fastball."

—*TOMMY JOHN, AFTER HIS BREAKTHROUGH RECONSTRUCTIVE ELBOW SURGERY*

"IT'S JUST BATTLE against battle. Who's gonna get the hit, or who's gonna get 'em out. That's all it is, is a battle."

—*MARK FIDRYCH, NO BIG DEAL*

"ALL YOU HAVE to do is pick up a baseball.
It begs to you: Throw me."

—*PITCHER DAVE DRAVECKY, COMEBACK*

"IT WAS A CROSS between a screwball and a changeup.
It was a screw-up."

—*CUBS RELIEVER BOB PATTERSON ON A LOUSY PITCH HIT BY CINCINNATI'S BARRY LARKIN OFF HIM FOR A GAME-WINNING HOMER, FROM THE WALL STREET JOURNAL, QUOTED IN PARADE, DECEMBER 29, 1996*

FIDRYCH'S 15 MINUTES

THE DEGENERATION OF A HITTER is usually a slow process, often taking several years of declining batting averages for the scenario to play out. Pitching offers far less subtlety.

There are occasionally hurlers who lose their ability to throw hard, adapt, and get years more resourcefulness out of their careers, but far more simply wake up one morning with an arm that can no longer handle the strains of their profession. Age often has nothing to do with it; a 20-year-old can hear a frightful "pop" on the mound and be finished no matter what muscles or reflexes he possesses. With this in mind, it is no surprise good pitching seems so hard to come by—and even harder to make last.

Mark Fidrych was 21 years old in the spring of 1976, his name unknown to all but the most ardent followers of the hapless Detroit Tigers. He had experienced some success in the minors the previous year, but he was not on Detroit's major-league roster during spring training. Even after making the club, he made just two relief appearances the first six weeks of the season. It was thought he needed more seasoning, but with the team sinking fast, Tigers manager Ralph Houk decided to let the kid start May 15 in Cleveland. Less than two hours later, Fidrych had a 2-1 victory, Houk a young pitching ace, and baseball its newest hero.

Possessing excellent control and a genuine enthusiasm for the game, Fidrych was prone to running up and shaking hands with his infielders after nice plays, landscaping the pitching mound, and even talking to the ball. Tall and thin, his hair a mass of blond curls, he was nicknamed "The Bird" (after the Sesame Street character Big Bird) and quickly became the biggest gate attraction in the majors. He started the All-Star Game and by year's end was 19-9 with a league-leading 2.34 ERA and 24 complete games in just 29 starts. Young, strong, and healthy, he looked like a lock for a dozen more years of stardom.

The next spring, he suddenly developed tendinitis in his arm. Years struggling to recapture his previous form produced just a 10-10 record, and he was finished by 1980. Nobody had seen him coming, and in the end he was gone just as fast.

"BEST PITCHER I ever had, period. You rolled the ball across the clubhouse floor and he'd grab it and pitch."

—SPARKY ANDERSON ON JACK MORRIS

"MADDUX IS A FIERCE COMPETITOR, great pitcher, great fielder, student of the game, and a nasty little bugger, too."

—ATLANTA MANAGER BOBBY COX ON GREG MADDUX,
BASEBALL DIGEST, JANUARY 1996

OUTSIDE THE LINES

"I NEVER QUESTIONED the integrity of an umpire. Their eyesight, yes."

—LEO DUROCHER, NICE GUYS FINISH LAST

THREE PLAYERS, ONE CARD

BEFORE THE BUSINESS of collecting baseball cards became a big business, there were not dozens of manufacturers putting out everything from gold-tipped cards to holographic images of stars in action. There was only one real card company that mattered—Topps—and every kid was out to get the same players and the same rock-hard gum as each new series was released throughout the summer. Not nearly as glamorous or flashy as today's cards, those of decades past seemed to have more character even if their shortcomings were more evident.

If a player was traded too late for a picture to be taken of him in his new uniform, there was no computerized method for fixing things; a new cap and jersey were simply painted over the old photo by artists whose workmanship was not exactly up to Picasso's. Rookies didn't earn their own cards before ever playing a game, as even high school draft picks do today; instead they shared space with one, two, or even three other hopefuls. We were left to wonder which third baseman would make it—Mike Schmidt, Ron Cey, or Dave Hilton—and sometimes waited years for an answer.

Even the players themselves seemed to have more fun with

cards then, batting or pitching from the wrong direction while posing for unsuspecting photographers. In 1969, Aurelio Rodriguez of the Angels pulled the biggest prank of all when he had a batboy pose for his card. This probably could not happen in today's high-tech world, and it's really too bad. Where have you gone, Dave Hilton?

"I CAN REMEMBER a reporter asking for a quote, and I didn't know what a quote was. I thought it was some kind of soft drink."

—*JOE DiMAGGIO*

"I LIKE THE JOB I have now, but if I had my life to live over again, I'd like to have ended up a sports writer."

—*RICHARD NIXON, PRESIDENT OF THE UNITED STATES AT THE TIME*

"THE FIRST RULE for sports announcers might well hold true for the patrons in the park: Follow the ball. But this rule should be broken, or modified, to suit the occasion."

—*HALL OF FAME BROADCASTER RED BARBER, EXPLAINING HOW TO WATCH A BASEBALL GAME*

"THE KRANK: His Language and What It Means."

—*TITLE OF BOOK ON THE STRANGE VERBIAGE AND ACTIONS OF BASEBALL'S EARLIEST FANS—OR "KRANKS," AROUND 1880*

". . . JUMPED ABOUT LIKE COLTS, stamped their feet, clapped their hands, threw their hats in the air, slapped their companions on the back, winked knowingly . . . and from a baseball standpoint, enjoyed themselves tremendously."

—NEW YORK TIMES *ACCOUNT OF FANS AT A* GIANTS *GAME,* MAY 31, 1888

"VERILY, BROOKLYN IS FAST earning the title of the 'City of Baseball Clubs' as well as the 'City of Churches.' As numerous as are its church spires, pointing the way to heaven, the present prospect indicates that they may soon be outnumbered by the rapidly increasing ball clubs."

—NEW YORK CITY NEWSPAPER, 1856

"SCORES RUSHED into the nearest saloon to take a drink on it; prohibition men . . . plunged recklessly into buttermilk. . . . Men were laughing, girls . . . giggling, boys . . . yelling, horses braying, dogs barking . . . in one cloudburst of happiness that ought to have cured all the

gout, rheumatism, dyspepsia and putrefied
livers in . . . the best State in the Union."

—*Description of Orioles fans celebrating their team's
clinching of the 1894 pennant, Baltimore Sun,
September 25, 1894*

"Hundreds who could or would not produce the
necessary fifty cents for admission looked on through
cracks in the fence, or even climbed boldly to the top,
while others were perched in the topmost limbs of the
trees or on roofs of surrounding houses."

—*Harper's Weekly account of 1870 game between the
visiting Cincinnati Red Stockings (winners of 92 straight
games) and Brooklyn Atlantics*

"Well, I don't know anything about base ball, or town
ball, now-a-days, but it does me good to see these fellows.
They've done something to add to the glory of our city."

—*Views of a fan rooting for the Cincinnati Red Stockings,
(Cincinnati) Commercial, July 1, 1869*

WET PAINT

OPENING DAY IS MEANT to provide a fresh start for ballclubs, but there is at least one case where things were a little too fresh for comfort. Management for the Boston Braves had spruced up their ballpark with a new coat of paint just before the 1946 season, then drew 18,261 for the home opener against the Dodgers. What they realized too late was that the paint on many of the refurbished seats had not yet dried, and approximately 5,000 infuriated fans left the park with green blotches on their coats and pants. Thinking quickly, Braves publicity director Billy Sullivan arranged for "An Apology to Braves Fans" to run in Boston papers, with the club offering to pay all cleaning expenses for damaged clothes. Bills came in from as far away as California, Nebraska, and Florida—13,000 of them in all—and the incident wound up costing the organization nearly $6,000. Still, fans appreciated the effort, and once things dried up the club set an attendance record that summer.

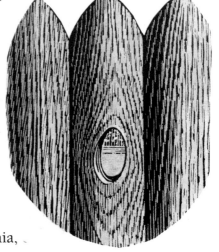

"IF THERE IS ANY one effort that clubs ought to make more than another to promote the popularity of our game and to ensure its respectability, it is the one to encourage the patronage of the fair sex."

—*EDITOR OF* MAYER'S CHRONICLE, *1867*

". . . CHAMPIONSHIP MATCHES will draw a better average attendance . . . the public will feel confident that strong men will meet."

— *ALBERT* SPALDING, (CHICAGO) TRIBUNE, FEBRUARY *13, 1876*

"I DON'T KNOW that it's so important to have Tug McGraw's autograph. It's not like he's Donald Duck or something."

—*ELEMENTARY SCHOOL GIRL ON MEETING* TUG MCGRAW *AT HIS CHILDREN'S SCHOOL,* SPORTS ILLUSTRATED, NOVEMBER *20, 1978*

"THE BASEBALL FAN comes in every size and shape. It is not surprising that in Los Angeles, where religious sects of outrageous and neurotic extremes are embarrassingly common, some baseball fans go batty."

—*JIM* BROSNAN, PENNANT RACE

"You do things my way, or meet me after the game."

—Manager Frank Chance's supposed warning to his Cubs players to get their attention

"Don't pull that stuff on me. How can a pipsqueak like you be Babe Ruth's manager?"

—Doorman to 5'5" Yankees skipper Miller Huggins

". . . you could look up into the upper deck and recognize your mother, the stands were so close to the field."

—Pee Wee Reese on Ebbets Field

"It gets late early out there."

—Yogi Berra on the tough late-inning shadows in Yankee Stadium's left field

"On turf the ball comes to me and says, 'Catch me.' On grass it says, 'Look out, sucker.'"

—Greg Pryor, Playing the Field

"Fenway Park in Boston is a lyric little bandbox of a ballpark. Everything is painted green and seems in curiously sharp focus, like the inside of an old-fashioned peeping-type Easter egg.

—JOHN UPDIKE, THE NEW YORKER

"It's the only way I knew to fill Shibe Park."

—CRACK BY YANKEES MANAGER JOE MCCARTHY ON 295-POUND PITCHER WALTER "JUMBO" BROWN, WHO HE OFTEN PITCHED IN PHILADELPHIA'S SPARSELY POPULATED BALLPARK, THE SPORTING NEWS, AUGUST 29, 1964

"We lived too far from Brooklyn in those days to get the day games on the radio, but when the Dodgers played night games I'd stay up with my ears glued to the set. That's what made it unbelievable to me when the Dodgers gave me a tryout in 1950 and signed me to a contract."

—PITCHER JOHNNY PODRES, WHO WON THE CLINCHING GAME IN THE 1955 WORLD SERIES FOR BROOKLYN'S ONLY SERIES CHAMPION, BASEBALL DIGEST, OCTOBER 1973

ONE SHORT OF A MILLION

OVER A 12-YEAR MAJOR-LEAGUE CAREER during which he became known for his method of declaring baserunners out with his "shotgun" finger rather than for his game-calling skills, umpire Ron Luciano made many friends (and a few enemies) among the players of his day. Only once, however, did he admit to helping a baserunner, and he did so with good reason. Baseball was running a promotion in 1975 around the scoring of the one millionth run in big-league history, and whichever teams and umpires were involved in the game where the run was scored would be given free engraved watches. Ron was never one to pass up a good deal.

Luciano was working third base in an A's-White Sox game when word came that the 999,999th run had been scored in another contest. There was a man on third with nobody out at the time, and as Luciano later revealed in his book *The Umpire Strikes Back*, "I could hear that snazzy timepiece ticking on my wrist. I could feel the gold against my skin." The batter lifted a short fly to right, and despite Ron's pleas to stay put, the man on third tagged up and was thrown out at the plate. The man on first had advanced to second, however, offering one more chance at paydirt. A line-drive single followed, but the lead runner inexplicably turned on the breaks as he reached third. "Go! Go!" Luciano screamed, but it was too late. Just then it was announced to the crowd that Houston's Bob Watson had scored the millionth run elsewhere, and the ever-optimistic ump could be heard yelling to players at the end of the inning, "Come on, let's go. Only 999,999 more to go."

"WE ROOTED for the Dodgers because they had black players. If we rooted for anyone else, we got the ---- beat out of us."

—*REGGIE JACKSON, RECALLING THE FAVORITE TEAM OF HIS CHILDHOOD, BASEBALL DIGEST, JANUARY 1974*

"WHEN I SAID the hardest thing for me to leave behind was baseball games, I was eyed as a nut of some kind. I'm not sure that anyone understood, but when you have baseballs for red corpuscles, you don't give up the game without a constriction of the blood vessels."

—*SISTER MARY BARBARA BROWN, C.S.C., OF SAN FRANCISCO, WHO BECAME A NUN THE SAME YEAR (1936) THAT JOE DIMAGGIO LEFT TOWN TO PLAY FOR THE YANKEES*

"**W**HAT ARE YOU crying for? We won 4-0."

—*Tom Seaver to his wife, Nancy, following his one-hit win over Chicago, July 9, 1969; Seaver had lost a perfect game with one out in the ninth inning, Baseball Digest, November 1974*

"**W**E WHO ARE ABOUT to Cry Salute You."

—*Sign hanging from the left-field stands at Shea Stadium on the night Willie Mays said goodbye to baseball and his fans, September 1973*

"**L**ORD, I'D GIVE my right arm for an ice-cold beer."
"So would the Babe."

—*Exchange between Joe Dugan and Waite Hoyt as they helped carry Babe Ruth's coffin out of St. Patrick's Cathedral and into the sweltering August heat of Manhattan, 1948*

"**N**O, I SUPPOSE NOT—but who can?"

—*One-armed outfielder Pete Gray, when asked if he could hit Bob Feller, Baseball Digest, May 1971*

"I DON'T REMEMBER your name, but you were a sucker
for a high inside fastball."

—FORMER YANKEE CATCHER BILL DICKEY TO ANOTHER OLD-TIMER
WHO HAD SPOTTED HIM IN AN ELEVATOR AND SAID HELLO,
BASEBALL DIGEST, JULY 1971

"ONLY IF SHE were digging in."

—EARLY WYNN, NOTORIOUS BRUSH-BACK PITCHER, ON WHETHER HE
WOULD USE SUCH TACTICS ON HIS OWN MOTHER

"EVERY BIG-LEAGUER and his wife should teach their children
to pray: 'God bless Mommy, God bless Daddy,
and God bless Babe Ruth.'"

—RUTH TEAMMATE WAITE HOYT, BASEBALL AS I HAVE KNOWN IT

"IF WE'RE GOING to have any clowns
on this team, it's going to be me."

—BROOKLYN MANAGER CASEY STENGEL, DEMANDING THAT FUN-
LOVING FRENCHY BORDAGARAY SHAVE THE BEARD AND
MUSTACHE HE HAD GROWN FOR KICKS

THE SPACEMAN

Asked to assess the 1975 World Series after the Red Sox and Cincinnati Reds split the first two games, Boston pitcher Bill Lee paused as reporters adjusted their pencils and tape recorders. Then he issued his accurate and succinct reply: "Tied."

The response was typical of the flaky left-hander, whose unpredictable wit made him a fan favorite and a thorn in the side of management. He admitted sprinkling marijuana on his buckwheat pancakes, frequently jogged (before the fad) the eight miles from his home to Fenway Park, and called puffy-cheeked Red Sox manager Don Zimmer a "gerbil." Traded by Zimmer and Co. to Montreal, Lee grew a Rip Van Winkle-esque beard, made the disabled list twice—once after being hit by a cab while jogging, once for falling 10 feet trying to climb the outside wall of a lady friend's apartment—and was let go for good after protesting the release of friend Rodney Scott by ripping his uniform to shreds and leaving it on manager Jim Fanning's desk. "Spaceman" signed his own release papers: "Bill Lee, Earth '82."

"IT TOOK EIGHT hours . . . seven and a half to find the heart."

—STEVE MCCATTY ON HEARING OF CHARLIE O. FINLEY'S HEART
SURGERY, TEMPORARY INSANITY

"MY FAVORITE UMPIRE is a dead one."

—JOHNNY EVERS

". . . NO HIGHER COMPLIMENT can be paid to a member
of the fraternity then to select him to act as umpire in a
first-class contest, as such choice implies . . . confidence
in his knowledge of the rules . . . and in his ability to
enforce them resolutely."

—HENRY CHADWICK, PUTTING HIS VIEW OF UMPS IN THE EARLY
NATIONAL LEAGUE IN WRITING, AROUND 1880

"WHEN I BROKE IN, they didn't keep track of things the way
they do now. These days they have a stat for how many
times a guy goes for a cup of coffee."

—MARK MCGWIRE ON THE HABIT OF SPORTS WRITERS CHARTING
THE DISTANCE OF HIS HOME RUNS, SPORTS ILLUSTRATED,
AUGUST 26, 1996

"THE UMPIRING of the game by Mr. Chandler was fair and impartial, notwithstanding the growling which was to be expected from a New York club."

—BOSTON HERALD *SPORTS WRITER, GETTING IN A BARB AT HIS TEAM'S OPPOSITION, MAY 13, 1872*

"NEVER CHANGE a decision, never stop to talk to a man. Make 'em play ball and keep their mouths shut, and . . . people will be on your side and you'll be called the king of umpires."

—*PLAYER AND MANAGER-TURNED-UMPIRE BOB FERGUSON, AROUND 1890*

"MANY BASEBALL FANS look at an umpire as a sort of necessary evil to the luxury of baseball, like the odor that follows an automobile."

—CHRISTY MATHEWSON

"IS THE BASE BALL Player a Chattel?"

—*TITLE OF AN ESSAY BY STAR PLAYER JOHN MONTGOMERY WARD SHORTLY AFTER THE 1887 SALE OF KING KELLY TO BOSTON*

"I'M SURE, I'm positive, I know there were people who changed their lives because of the Miracle Mets. People felt better. It was a good thing."

—*FORMER METS INFIELDER ED CHARLES*

"HERE LIES A MAN who batted .300."

—*WHAT CAP ANSON WANTED PUT ON HIS TOMBSTONE; HIS LIFETIME AVERAGE WAS ..329*

"I NEVER HAD TO BE lonely behind the plate, where I could talk to hitters. I also learned that by engaging them in conversation, I could sometimes distract them."

—*CATCHER ROY CAMPANELLA, IT'S GOOD TO BE ALIVE*

"THE ONE THING that sticks out in my mind was to be a pitcher's best friend. The most important part of the job is often the part you can't see."

—*FORMER CATCHER TIM MCCARVER ON THE ART OF THE POSITION*

THE 49-YEAR WAIT

FORTY-NINE YEARS IS A LONG TIME to wait for anything, but for Washington Senators fans the years from 1926 to 1975 must have seemed like an eternity. Not only did the club go that entire span without winning a pennant, but it had already left town for Arlington, Texas, when its rooters were finally able to hear from the source whether or not Senators right fielder Sam Rice had indeed caught a fly ball hit by Pittsburgh's Earl Smith in the third game of the 1925 World Series.

Until Carlton Fisk was accused of interfering with Ed Armbrister in the 1975 fall classic, Rice's dive into the right-center field stands to rob Smith of a homer was the most disputed call in Series history. The Pirates and defending-champion Senators had split the first two games in Pittsburgh, and the Series moved to the nation's capital for the next three contests. President and Mrs. Coolidge were among the 36,493 packing Griffith's Stadium for Game 3, and the Senators had a 4-3 lead in the top of the eighth when Smith crushed his deep shot to right.

The speedy Rice started back in quick pursuit, grabbing hold of the ball just as he hit the three-foot-high fence in right-center and fell over into the crowd seated behind it. At least 10 seconds passed before he emerged, showing umpires the ball inside his glove. Pirates players protested that hometown fans had placed the ball back in Rice's mitt after it fell free during his fall, and many Pittsburgh rooters in the crowd offered affidavits claiming the same. The Senators won 4-3, and although they later lost the Series in seven games, Rice was forever hounded about whether he had made the catch. His only comment: "The umpire called him out, didn't he?"

Four decades passed, and eventually Rice had a change of heart. He wrote out his own description of the play, then sealed it in an envelope labeled "to be opened after my death." Rice died at age 84 in October 1974, and early the following year the letter was read aloud before witnesses by Paul Kerr, president of the Hall of Fame. It stated, in part: "I turned slightly to my right and had the ball in view all the way, going at top speed and about 15 feet from the bleachers jumped as high as I could and back handed and the ball hit the center of pocket in glove (I had a death grip on it). . . . I toppled over on my stomach into first row of bleachers, I hit my Adam's apple on something which sort of knocked me out for a few seconds but [center fielder Earl] McNeely arrived about that time and grabbed me by the shirt and pulled me out. . . . At no time did I lose possession of the ball."

"If I'd known I was gonna pitch a no-hitter today,
I would have gotten a haircut."

—Bo Belinsky, The Suitors of Spring

"I never shave on days I'm gonna pitch. I try to look extra
mean on those days. It helps me get batters out."

—Cleveland fireballer Sam McDowell,
The Suitors of Spring

"Joe, it's been a while. Do the batters still get three strikes?"

—Red Sox catcher Moe Berg to manager Joe Cronin upon
making a rare appearance in a game, The Picture History of
the Boston Red Sox

"The old-style baseball cleats we wore had an innersole
inside. I ripped that out. I always had to have about 10 pairs
of shoes—size 9, a size and a half smaller than my dress
shoes—because after a while, the spikes would come
through the sole into my feet."

—Maury Wills on making his shoes lighter to add speed,
On the Run

"I NEVER RAN from signs; I ran on my own. Any good baserunner has to be on his own."

—GEORGE CASE, WHO LED THE AMERICAN LEAGUE IN STEALS FIVE STRAIGHT YEARS, BASEBALL BETWEEN THE LINES

"HE TOOK GREAT delight in fielding a base hit in right field with a man on first base and pausing. He'd just stand there, sometimes in deep right, and hold the ball saying, 'Go ahead to third.' Runners wouldn't dare go because Clemente nailed them every time."

—MAURY WILLS ON ROBERTO CLEMENTE, ON THE RUN

"I DON'T CARE or not whether it is childish. Long before I possessed any capacity to examine myself or the reason for the game's appeal to me, I loved it."

—NOVELIST JAMES T. FARRELL ON BASEBALL, OUR GAME

"WELL, MR. BARROW, Lou Gehrig is badly underpaid."

—JOE DIMAGGIO'S RESPONSE WHEN YANKEE GENERAL MANAGER ED BARROW TOLD JOE THAT HIS 1937 CONTRACT DEMAND OF $45,000 FOLLOWING HIS ROOKIE SEASON WAS HIGHER THAN THE $41,000 GEHRIG MADE AFTER 12 YEARS

BALLOT-STUFFING

Each time player selection for the All-Star Game has been turned over to the fans, there have been complaints of popularity playing a larger role than talent in who gets picked. Ballots are handed out at ballparks in each major-league city, prompting many fans to simply punch in the names of players from the home team—regardless of how they are performing that season.

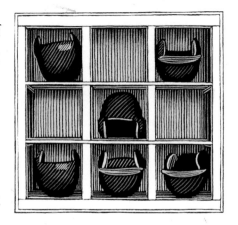

Never was the problem of hometown ballot-stuffing more evident than in 1957, when seven members of the fourth-place Cincinnati Reds were selected to represent the National League squad. It seems a Cincinnati newspaper printed up ballots that were already filled out, then told fans where to send them. Commissioner Ford Frick eventually stepped in and dropped two Reds from the squad, and not until 1970 were fans allowed to vote again. The NL team with the most All-Stars during the 1970s? Who else—the Cincinnati Reds.

"These are the saddest of possible words:
'Tinker to Evers to Chance.'

Trio of bear cubs and fleeter than birds,
Tinker and Evers and Chance."

—POEM BY NEW YORK WORLD *REPORTER*
FRANKLIN P. ADAMS, *1908*

"PLAYERS HAVE HURTS and fears and anxieties. As an
announcer, I'm strictly for the underdog."

—CATCHER-TURNED-BROADCASTER JOE GARAGIOLA,
THE SPORTING NEWS, *APRIL 4, 1962*

"IT WAS SO WONDERFUL, Joe.
You never heard such cheering."
"Yes, I have."

—EXCHANGE BETWEEN NEWLYWEDS MARILYN MONROE AND
JOE DIMAGGIO ON MONROE'S RETURN FROM KOREA, WHERE
SHE HAD ENTERTAINED SOME *100,000* ARMY TROOPS

"WHAT'S THE MATTER, son? Did you lose your mother?"
"No, sir, I lost my fastball."

—EXCHANGE BETWEEN A PRIEST AND EX-ALL-STAR GENE CONLEY
AFTER CONLEY HAD BEEN SHELLED BY MINOR-LEAGUERS *IN A*
COMEBACK ATTEMPT, THE PITCHER

DIAMOND GEMS

JOE BAUMAN set a professional baseball record with 72 home runs for the Roswell (New Mexico) Rockets of the Class C Longhorn League in 1954. But he never played in the majors.

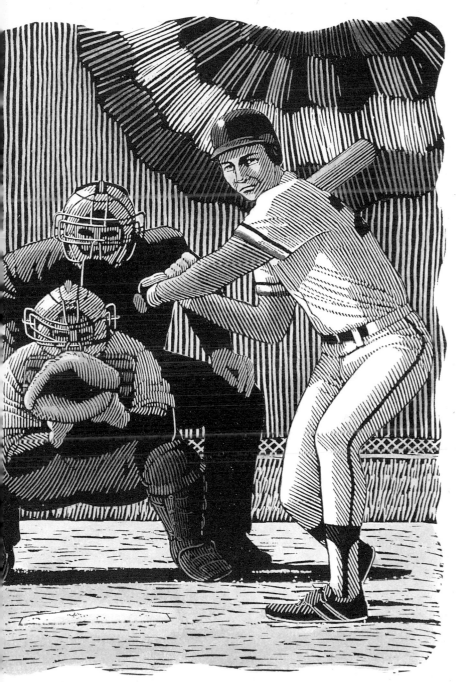

SHE FANNED THE BABE

THOUGH BABE RUTH and Lou Gehrig were two of baseball's greatest hitters, a woman once struck them out. It happened in 1932, when the Yankees stopped in Chattanooga en route home from spring training camp. Joe Engel, owner of the independent team there, had a widespread reputation for innovative ideas, but this one was the topper. He unveiled a local pitching phenomenon named Jackie Mitchell. She proceeded to strike out Ruth, Gehrig, and fellow slugger Tony Lazzeri—a feat that made national headlines.

JOE NUXHALL was 15 years and 10 months old when he worked two-thirds of an inning for the Cincinnati Reds against the St. Louis Cardinals on June 10, 1944. He was the youngest player ever to appear in the majors.

BROOKLYN FANS of 1920 ate nickel hot dogs and read nickel programs. Schoolchildren got bleacher seats for a quarter apiece on Friday afternoons.

THE 1970 PITTSBURGH pitching staff might have been mistaken for a butcher shop. It included players named Moose, Lamb, and Veale.

Nick Altrock (1898-1933) and Minnie Minoso
(1949-80) were the only men to play major-league
baseball in five different decades.

Late in the 1990 campaign, Ken Griffey Sr. and Ken Griffey
Jr. became the only father-son tandem to play together.
They played next to each other, as the left and center fielder
for the Seattle Mariners, and also batted in succession, second and third. Griffey Sr. was then 40, twice his son's age.

Arf Arf Arf!

During his tenure as owner of the St. Louis Browns, Bill
Veeck always needed money for basic expenses. He tried to
convince Cleveland general manager Hank Greenberg to
buy first baseman Hank Arft, but the Indians already had
Luke Easter at the position. In his final plea, Veeck's tele-
type jammed and printed: "ARFARFARFARFARFARFARF."
Greenberg wired back: "I can't stop laughing. Keep that dog
in St. Louis."

Hank and Tommie Aaron combined for more home runs
than any other brother combination. Their total of 768
included 13 by Tommie, a regular only as a rookie (1962).

A ZIPPED LIP

DURING HIS LONG CAREER as player, coach, and manager, Leo Durocher built a reputation as a champion umpire baiter. Coaching at first one day, Leo the Lip began jawboning from the minute the game began. Finally, umpire George Magerkurth warned him he'd be ejected if he said another word. Seeking to avoid ejection from the close game, Durocher stopped talking. On the very next play, however, Pete Reiser was called out at first on a close call. Durocher disagreed but didn't say a word. Still, he wanted to let the Brooklyn fans know how he felt. So he pretended to faint, lying flat on the ground. Magerkurth repeated his out call, then pointed to Durocher and said, "Dead or alive, you're out, too!"

JOE DiMAGGIO, whose 56-game hitting streak is the longest in major-league history, had a longer streak in the minors. He hit in 61 straight contests while playing for the San Francisco Seals of the old Pacific Coast League.

JOE ADCOCK COMPILED a record 18 total bases in a single game when he hit four home runs and a double for the Milwaukee Braves against the Brooklyn Dodgers at Ebbets Field on July 31, 1954.

Harry Wright, once a cricket player, formed the first professional team, the Cincinnati Red Stockings, in 1869. The team went 69-0-1 that year and launched a 130-game winning streak that did not end until June 14, 1870.

Charlie Dressen had an ingenious way of catching curfew violators. At 1 A.M., he'd give the hotel elevator operator a new baseball and tell him to collect as many autographs as he could. Dressen promised he'd get the remainder of the team to sign the ball the next day.

The Houston Astros and Pittsburgh Pirates had a rain-in at the Astrodome on June 15, 1976. Torrential rains flooded the city, preventing the umpires, fans, and stadium personnel from reaching the ballpark, even though the two teams were present.

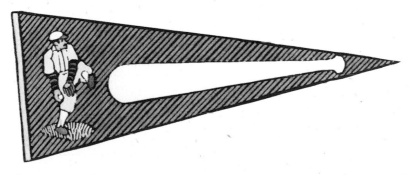

NO CRACKERS IN BED

EARLY IN THE CENTURY, teams assigned two players to a room on road trips. They sometimes had to share the same bed. That presented problems for the famous pitcher-catcher battery of Rube Waddell and Ossie Schreckengost. One spring, the latter complained to Athletics manager Connie Mack that he couldn't sleep with Waddell because the pitcher insisted upon eating Animal Crackers in bed. To satisfy the catcher, the next contract sent to Waddell contained a clause prohibiting him from eating in bed. It became known as the "Animal Crackers Contract."

BAD FINANCING and bad weather forced the expansion Seattle Pilots to become the Milwaukee Brewers after only one season (1969). Seattle got a second chance with another expansion club, the Mariners, in 1977.

NIGHT GAMES were banned in 1943 because of wartime blackout restrictions. That same year, the St. Louis Cardinals advertised for players after losing 200 athletes to military service.

BECAUSE CERTAIN CITIES banned Sunday games early in the century, major-league games were played in Canton,

Columbus, Dayton, and Toledo, Ohio; Fort Wayne, Indiana; Grand Rapids, Michigan; and Providence, Rhode Island.

DAVEY LOPES, second baseman of the Los Angeles Dodgers, was elected to the National League's All-Star starting lineup in 1981 despite a .169 batting average—worst in All-Star history.

WHEN THE CUBS beat the Phillies 26-23 on August 25, 1922, the two teams produced the most runs in a single game. The Boston Red Sox and Chicago White Sox share the record for most runs scored by a single team (29).

THE THREE ALOU BROTHERS—Felipe, Matty, and Jesus— batted in the same inning when the San Francisco Giants played the New York Mets at Shea Stadium in 1963. All three grounded out. It was the only time three brothers batted for the same team in the same inning.

DURING THE 1935 SEASON, only 88,113 fans turned out to watch the last-place St. Louis Browns.

A SCOOP OF COWHIDE

DURING HIS PLAYING DAYS with the Cardinals, Leo Durocher was once nailed by the hidden-ball trick. That night, he planned to dine with the manager of the St. Louis hotel where he was living. Knowing Leo liked chocolate ice cream, his host had two huge portions brought to the table. Durocher dug in with enthusiasm—until his spoon struck a solid object: a hidden ball.

THE ANGELS HAVE CHANGED their name three times without ever leaving Southern California. They were the Los Angeles Angels from 1961-64 and the California Angels from 1965-96 before becoming the Anaheim Angels for 1997.

Wɪᴛʜ ʜɪs Cʜɪᴄᴀɢᴏ Cᴜʙs trailing by nine runs one afternoon, manager Charlie Grimm, coaching at third base, dug a hole and buried his lineup card.

Hᴀɴᴋ Aᴀʀᴏɴ and Eddie Mathews hit more home runs during the time they were teammates with the Braves (863) than any other tandem in baseball history. Aaron and Mathews played together from 1954-66.

Wɪʟʟɪᴀᴍ Scʜʀɪᴠᴇʀ, catcher for the Chicago Cubs, was the first player to catch a ball thrown from the top of the Washington Monument, on August 25, 1894.

FUNNY GUY

Rᴇʟɪᴇꜰ ᴘɪᴛᴄʜᴇʀ Moe Drabowsky used practical jokes to escape the boredom of long days in the bullpen. A specialist at giving hot-foots, he imitated managers' voices so well that he could call opposing bullpens and order pitchers to warm up. He changed the numbers on hotel-room doors, ordered takeout food from Hong Kong, and put snakes in Luis Aparicio's pants pocket before the shortstop got to the clubhouse. Aparicio, deathly afraid of snakes, set an all-time record for getting undressed.

TIGHT WITH A BUCK

LONGTIME BASEBALL EXECUTIVE Branch Rickey earned a reputation as the father of the farm system, the man who integrated baseball, and the force behind baseball's first wave of expansion. He was also known for his reluctance to part with a dollar. During a reunion for his 1934 Gashouse Gang Cardinals, Rickey praised the participants as men who loved the game so much that they would have played for nothing. Pepper Martin couldn't resist. "Thanks to you, Mr. Rickey, we almost did!" he said.

DAVE KINGMAN homered for teams in all four divisions in 1977: the Mets (NL East), Giants (NL West), Yankees (AL East), and Angels (AL West). Central Divisions were added in 1994.

PITTSBURGH MANAGER FRANKIE FRISCH had a novel way of objecting to a game continuing in inclement weather: He marched out of the dugout clad in raincoat, rain hat, and galoshes while carrying a large umbrella. Not surprisingly, immediate ejection followed.

EBBETS FIELD ORGANIST Gladys Gooding earned her spurs the second day on the job: May 9, 1942. As umpires Bill

Stewart, Ziggy Sears, and Tom Dunn walked onto the field, Gooding burst into song with "Three Blind Mice."

WE WAS ROBBED!

AIRMEN AT GOWEN FIELD in Idaho during the '40s formed a baseball team to occupy their free time. One day, the airbase nine was engaged in a tight game against prisoners—and an umpire—from a nearby penitentiary. After a close decision went against him, Lt. Carl Robbins complained, "That's robbery!" An inmate answered, "What do you expect? That's what the umpire is in here for."

WITH BOTH TEAMS going nowhere and their managers about to be fired, the Cleveland Indians and Detroit Tigers traded managers in 1960. Joe Gordon went from Cleveland to Detroit for Jimmy Dykes in a midseason move that helped neither team.

LONGTIME SPORTSMAN'S PARK groundskeeper Bill Stockstick used a goat to help him trim the outfield grass for the St. Louis Cardinals.

LO TENGO!

RICHIE ASHBURN, center fielder for the original New York Mets in 1962, had a communications gap with Spanish-speaking shortstop Elio Chacon. So Ashburn learned the Spanish words for "I got it!" When a looping fly ball came his way later that day, Ashburn screamed, *"Lo tengo! Lo tengo!"* Chacon stopped in his tracks but left fielder Frank Thomas, who spoke no Spanish, knocked Ashburn aside just as he was reaching for the ball.

ELLIS BURKS and Hank Aaron are the only players in National League history to produce 200 hits, 40 home runs, and 30 stolen bases in the same season.

JOE NIEKRO hit his only major-league homer against brother Phil, beating him in a 1976 game. Together, the Niekros won more games (539) than any other pair of pitching brothers.

LEFTY GOMEZ INSISTED he knew the identity of a small white object found by Neil Armstrong when he first walked on the moon. According to Gomez, the object was a home run ball Jimmie Foxx hit against him in 1937.

ONE YEAR AFTER he set a major-league record with a home run per 8.5 at bats in 1995, Oakland's Mark McGwire tied the mark in 1996.

PEE WEE'S ACTING JOB

CLYDE KING ONCE GOT such a quick call from the Dodger bullpen that he didn't feel ready. When he asked for more warmup time, manager Charlie Dressen told shortstop Pee Wee Reese to put on a stalling act. The minute the umpire said "play ball," Reese called time, pretended to have something in his eye, and asked third baseman Billy Cox for "help." He was a bit too convincing, however. King—who was supposed to be getting loose on the mound—came over to tend to Reese instead.

PROPER CARE OF his bats helped Ty Cobb win a dozen batting crowns. He rubbed his bats for hours with the hollowed-out thigh of a steer, and he also treated them with tobacco juice in an effort to keep dampness out of the wood.

A Tip of the Cap

AFTER SIX SEASONS in Brooklyn, Casey Stengel was traded to Pittsburgh in 1918. Booed by the Ebbets Field faithful during his first trip to the plate as a Pirate, Stengel decided to win back his former fans. Seeing a sparrow caught on the outfield fence, he tucked the bird under his cap. When the crowd reacted with boos during his second at bat, Stengel called time, stepped back, and gave a sweeping bow— allowing the bird to escape.

WHEN BABE RUTH hit 29 home runs in 1919, he broke Gavvy Cravath's record of 24, set in 1915. Two years later, Ruth replaced Roger Connor as the career leader when he socked No. 138.

ONLY ONE NO-HITTER has been pitched on Opening Day: a 1-0 win by Cleveland's Bob Feller against the Chicago White Sox on April 16, 1940.

THE AMERICAN LEAGUE'S home run king was once traded for the batting champion. It happened on the eve of the 1960 season, when the Cleveland Indians traded Rocky Colavito to the Detroit Tigers for Harvey Kuenn.

I N 1928, the Hollywood Stars of the Pacific Coast League became the first team to travel by air.

TRADED FOR A FENCE

H ALL OF FAMER Lefty Grove got his start in the majors when he was traded for a center-field fence. The standout southpaw belonged to the Martinsburg, West Virginia, team when Jack Dunn, owner of the minor-league Baltimore Orioles, spotted him. Dunn learned that Martinsburg owed money for the erection of an outfield fence and offered to pay the bill in exchange for Grove. The pitcher went on to star for Baltimore before winning 300 games in the majors.

T HE BROOKLYN DODGERS, in search of greener pastures, played seven "home games" across the Hudson in Jersey City's Roosevelt Stadium in both 1956 and 1957.

A CTOR WILLIAM BENDIX, who played the title role in *The Babe Ruth Story,* was once Ruth's batboy.

S TAN MUSIAL never won a home run crown and Willie Mays never led in runs batted in.

NICE SHOT, UMP

To answer John McGraw's reference to him as "a blind robber," umpire Robert Emslie showed up at the Giants' practice with a rifle. He marched out to second base, split a match, and inserted a dime. Then he walked to home plate, aimed, and fired, sending the dime spinning into the outfield with his first shot. McGraw argued with him again—but never challenged his eyesight.

Ken Caminiti, Todd Hundley, and Mickey Mantle are the only switch-hitters to hit 40 home runs in a season. Mantle stood alone until Caminiti and Hundley joined him in 1996.

The second of Johnny Vander Meer's consecutive no-hitters coincided with the first night game at Brooklyn's Ebbets Field. With players not yet used to playing at night, the Cincinnati lefty sailed through the Dodger lineup on June 15, 1938.

The Detroit Tigers kept arguments to a minimum on July 14, 1972. The brother of catcher Tom Haller was plate umpire Bill Haller.

ALTHOUGH THE NATIONAL LEAGUE has refused to follow the American League's 1973 lead in adopting the designated hitter, the concept was first suggested by NL President John Heydler in 1928.

GENE TENACE, a little-known catcher with the 1972 Oakland Athletics, and Andruw Jones, a 19-year-old outfielder with the 1996 Atlanta Braves, are the only players to hit home runs in their first two World Series at bats.

AUNT MINNIE'S WINDOW

BEFORE THE ADVENT of television, baseball broadcasts depended on colorful announcers to captivate a listening audience. One of the best was Rosey Rowswell, voice of the Pittsburgh Pirates. With Ralph Kiner cracking frequent home runs for the ragtag Pirates, Rowswell got his audience to imagine a little old lady with an apartment window facing Forbes Field. Whenever a Kiner drive seemed headed for the seats, Rowswell yelled, "Open the window, Aunt Minnie, here it comes!" Then, as the ball left the park, he would smash a light bulb near the microphone.

THE HARWELL/DAPPER DEAL

A BROADCASTER was once traded for a catcher. Ernie Harwell was broadcasting for the minor-league Atlanta Crackers when Brooklyn general manager Branch Rickey, passing through town, happened to hear him. Rickey, needing an announcer to replace the ailing Red Barber, called Atlanta owner Earl Mann to ask for Harwell's release. Mann agreed only to exchange Harwell's contract for Cliff Dapper, a catcher with Brooklyn's Montreal farm club. Harwell has been a major-league broadcaster ever since.

BALTIMORE LEFT FIELDER John Lowenstein had a unique explanation for his hot hitting early in the 1982 season: He spent the time between innings flushing the clubhouse toilet to keep his wrists strong.

HERB WASHINGTON, a Michigan State track star, got into 105 major-league games without ever throwing a pitch or coming to bat. Used strictly as a pinch-runner by Charley Finley's world champion Oakland Athletics in 1974, Washington stole 29 bases in 45 attempts and scored 29 runs.

CONNIE MACK SPENT a record 50 seasons as manager of the Philadelphia Athletics. He was 88 when he finally retired.

KATHY 3, REGGIE 0

LIKE BABE RUTH, Reggie Jackson also whiffed while batting against a woman— only Jackson did it three times in one game! Kathy Arendsen, a 6'2", 170-pound right-hander, was the star soft-ball pitcher for the Raybestos Brakettes of Stratford, Connecticut. In 1981, she went 35-2 with 13 no-hitters and an ERA of 0.07 (that's right—Double-O-Seven). Arendsen threw several fastballs in excess of 95 mph during her exhibition game outing against the Yankee slugger.

EDDIE GAEDEL, the midget sent to bat as a publicity stunt by Bill Veeck's St. Louis Browns in 1951, wore an appropriate number: ⅛. Gaedel walked on four pitches—the sole extent of his baseball career.

THE NINTH MAN OUT

THE BLACK SOX SCANDAL of 1919 not only resulted in the lifetime suspensions of eight alleged participants— and the book and movie titled *Eight Men Out*—but suspension of a ninth player with knowledge of the World Series fix. Joe Gedeon, second baseman for the St. Louis Browns, was banned for betting on the Reds after learning the White Sox had been bribed to throw games.

BABE RUTH wore No. 3 because he was batting third in the Yankee lineup when the team decided to add numbers to its uniforms in 1929. Lou Gehrig, who batted behind him, drew No. 4.

ALTHOUGH TOM SEAVER, Nolan Ryan, and Doc Gooden did it after they left, no member of the New York Mets has ever pitched a no-hitter.

DETROIT FIRST BASEMAN Norm Cash, already a strikeout victim twice, tried to break up a Nolan Ryan no-hitter with a table leg in 1973. Cash came to the plate with the sawed-off leg of an old table in the clubhouse.

BATTING HELMETS were not in vogue when Cleveland's Ray Chapman was beaned by Yankee submariner Carl Mays during a game in 1920. Chapman, who died from his injuries, remains the only major-leaguer ever killed on the diamond.

PHIL WRIGLEY, owner of the Chicago Cubs, was angered when *Chicago Daily News* sports editor Lloyd Lewis ran a midseason box asking fans to vote for a new manager. Wrigley had to be restrained from running a Cub-sponsored ad asking for readers to choose a new sports editor.

ALTHOUGH RON BLOMBERG of the New York Yankees was the first designated hitter in 1973, Don Baylor of the 1979 California Angels was the first DH to win an MVP Award.

BECAUSE THE ADVENT of the DH rule prevented AL pitchers from batting after 1972, Baltimore's Roric Harrison remains the last AL hurler to hit a home run.

GET IN THE GAME, HACK

HACK WILSON HOLDS single-season records for runs batted in (190) and home runs by a National Leaguer (56) but none for playing the field. He sometimes passed the time in the outfield by talking to the fans. While talking to a fan in Philadelphia, Wilson hadn't noticed that Dodger manager Casey Stengel was changing pitchers. Walter Beck, angry at his departure, heaved the ball deep into the outfield. It crashed into the metal outfield fence like a clap of cymbals. Wilson, thinking the ball had been hit, grabbed it hastily and threw a strike to second base.

BOBBY BRAGAN was once ejected for offering orange juice to the umpires. He made the offering while bringing out the starting lineup to a game in 1957. Bragan, then Pittsburgh manager, had been ejected for arguing the day before.

PHILADELPHIA was the only city to produce two Triple Crown winners in the same season. Chuck Klein (Phillies) and Jimmie Foxx (Athletics) both won in their respective leagues in 1933.

UNRULY FANS STORMED onto the field in the last inning of the final game in Washington in 1971, causing the Senators to

forfeit a game they were winning. The team
became the Texas Rangers a year later.

ALTHOUGH THE 1930 PHILLIES had a .315 team batting
average, they finished dead last because of dreadful pitching
and defense. The team's ERA was 6.71, worst in baseball
history, while the fielders made 239 errors in 154 games.

PRESTON GOMEZ twice pinch-hit for pitchers who had
worked eight hitless innings. Both times, the bullpen blew
the game in the ninth. It happened with the 1971 Padres
(Clay Kirby) and 1974 Astros (Don Wilson).

WHILE HITTING A RECORD 61 homers for the New York
Yankees during the 1961 season, Roger Maris never
received an intentional walk; Mickey Mantle
was batting behind him.

WHEN NORMAL SHORE ROUTES were washed out
by the New England hurricane of 1938, the New York
Giants used an overnight steamboat to get to Boston
for a series with the Braves.

FOWL BALL

BEFORE THE TORONTO SKYDOME opened in 1989, the Blue Jays played in Exhibition Stadium, an open-air ballpark not far from the shores of Lake Ontario. When a flock of ducks landed on the field during a game between the Yankees and Blue Jays, rookie broadcaster Fran Healy told his New York audience, "That's the first time I've ever seen a fowl in fair territory."

THE 1945 WASHINGTON SENATORS failed to hit a single ball over the fence in their home park. Of the team's 28 home runs that season, 27 came on the road while one was Joe Kuhel's inside-the-park shot at Washington's Griffith Stadium.

WEAK-HITTING DETROIT SHORTSTOP Cesar Gutierrez was wearing No. 7 when he became the first modern player to go 7-for-7 in a game (12 innings) in 1970. The jersey had been given to him by mistake after the death of its former wearer, manager Charlie Dressen.

MARTY MARION, star shortstop for the St. Louis Cardinals, did not walk for a year when he fell off a cliff as a youngster.

THE 1899 CLEVELAND SPIDERS, a National League entry, won 20 and lost 134 for a .130 "winning" percentage—the worst ever recorded.

SINCE THE ALL-STAR VOTE was returned to the fans in 1970, only two write-in candidates have been elected to the starting lineup: National Leaguers Rico Carty, an outfielder, in 1970 and Steve Garvey, a first baseman, in 1974.

IN THE DOGHOUSE

CENTER FIELD WAS SO DISTANT in Griffith Stadium that the Washington Senators kept the American flag in a small doghouse-type box in fair territory. During a game against the Athletics, a Senator's long drive buried itself in the box. Philadelphia's Socks Seibold searched feverishly but couldn't find it, allowing the batter to circle the bases with an inside-the-doghouse home run.

CHUCK KLEIN of the Phillies edged Mel Ott of the Giants for the NL's 1929 home run crown partly because Philadelphia pitchers walked Ott five times—once with the bases loaded—in the last game of the season. Klein finished with 43 homers, one more than Ott.

TOYING WITH THE HITTER

DIZZY DEAN ONCE TOLD his catcher to drop a foul pop. The great but eccentric Cardinal star had bet a friend that he could strike out Vince DiMaggio four straight times. He was working on No. 4 when DiMaggio popped up. The catcher obliged his pitcher—infuriating St. Louis manager Frankie Frisch—but Dean completed the strikeout, winning the grand total of $80.

DALE LONG of the 1956 Pirates and Don Mattingly of the 1987 Yankees share the major-league record of hitting home runs in eight consecutive games.

RIP COLLINS of the Cardinals hated to throw away broken bats. Instead, he brought them home and converted them into a unique picket fence in front of his house.

DARRYL STRAWBERRY is the only man to play for all four teams that originated in New York: the Yankees, Dodgers, Giants, and Mets.

FRED LYNN hit the only grand-slam in the history of the All-Star Game. It came against Atlee Hammaker in the 50th Anniversary All-Star Game, held at Chicago's Comiskey Park in 1983.

WHAT A WAY TO END IT

ON MAY 26, 1959, Pirate lefty Harvey Haddix pitched 12 perfect innings against the Braves at Milwaukee County Stadium but lost the game in the 13th. Felix Mantilla was safe on an error by third baseman Don Hoak, Eddie Mathews bunted him to second, and Hank Aaron was purposely passed. Joe Adcock then hit the ball over the wall but Aaron, surprised at the sudden ending, veered directly from second base to the dugout. Adcock, in his home run trot, was ruled out for passing a runner. Mantilla was credited with scoring the only run of the game.

JOHNNY MIZE is the only player to have at least 50 homers but less than 50 strikeouts in the same season. He had 51 homers and 42 strikeouts for the 1947 New York Giants.

AL BENTON was the only pitcher to face both Babe Ruth and Mickey Mantle in regular-season American League games.

Bᴏʙᴏ Hᴏʟʟᴏᴍᴀɴ of the St. Louis Browns no-hit the Philadelphia Athletics in his starting debut on May 6, 1953, but never pitched another complete game in the majors.

Fʀᴏᴍ 1961-65, the Chicago Cubs operated without a manager. Decisions were made by a rotating board of "head coaches."

Jᴇꜰꜰ Kɪɴɢ is the only player to hit two home runs in an inning in back-to-back seasons. He did it for the Pittsburgh Pirates in 1995 and 1996.

Lᴏɴɢ ʙᴇꜰᴏʀᴇ Fʀᴀɴᴋ Tʜᴏᴍᴀꜱ, Yankee pitcher Stan Williams was known as "The Big Hurt." He got the nickname during his first road trip with the team—when he accidentally spiked the barefoot Mickey Mantle in an adjacent toilet stall.

Pɪᴛᴛꜱʙᴜʀɢʜ'ꜱ Rᴇɴɴɪᴇ Sᴛᴇɴɴᴇᴛᴛ went 7-for-7 in a nine-inning game as the Pirates beat the Cubs 22-0 in baseball's most lopsided shutout, on September 16, 1975.